About the Author

MERRITT is the Editor of *Bird Watching Magazine*, award-winning poet. His work has been published in USA and Australia, and he is the Poetry Editor of the magazine *Under the Radar*. His writing is inspired by a long interest in the natural world, in particular birds and ornithology. He blogs at polyolbion.blogspot.co.uk

By the same author:

Making the Most of the Light
Troy Town
hydrodaktulopsychicharmonica
The Elephant Tests

MATT MERRITT

A Sky Full of Birds

In Search of
Britain's Great Bird
Gatherings

LONDON · SYDNEY · AUCKLAND · JOHANNESBURG

1 3 5 7 9 10 8 6 4 2

Rider, an imprint of Ebury Publishing,
20 Vauxhall Bridge Road,
London SW1V 2SA

Rider is part of the Penguin Random House group of companies
whose addresses can be found at global.penguinrandomhouse.com

Copyright © Matt Merritt 2016

Matt Merritt has asserted his right to be identified as the author of this Work in
accordance with the Copyright, Designs and Patents Act 1988

First published by Rider in 2016. This edition published in 2017

www.penguin.co.uk

A CIP catalogue record for this book is available from the British Library

ISBN 9781846044809

Printed and bound by Clays Ltd, St Ives PLC

Penguin Random House is committed to a sustainable future
for our business, our readers and our planet. This book is made from
Forest Stewardship Council® certified paper.

For Natalie, Charlotte, Jacob and all my family,
with thanks for their endless patience

Contents

0   50   100 miles

0   50 100 150   200 km

N

1a Nethy Bridge

6a Bass Rock

12b Berwick-on-Tweed   **6c** The Farne Islands

6b Rathlin Island

5 The Tyne Bridge, Newcastle

6d Bempton Cliffs RSPB

7d York Minster

9 Spurn Point

11 Newborough   **4** Parkgate RSPB
Warren

1c Whitwick,   **15** Titchwell   **16** Cley
my home

1b Clwyd Moors   **14** Snettisham

8 Rutland Water,
home of Birdfair   **12a** Welney WWT

7c Stokenchurch

7a Tate Modern,
London

7b Ogmore-by-Sea   **13** Esher
Rugby Club

10 Somerset Levels   **2** Knepp
Castle Estate

3 Pagham Harbour

Bird gatherings described in each chapter

MAGNETITE

We are not so much of the earth,
even, as the most microscopic jewel-toothed chiton,
the single-minded sperm whale, the Atlantic salmon.
Even the birds. Especially the birds.

They are tethered by the same element
that silvers the backs of their eyes, the lodestones that stud
their skulls, or spines, while we wander song-lines, desire-lines,
remake maps, charts, the base metal of our words.

Matt Merritt

Introduction

I'm on my way down the M5, heading for Cornwall in the wettest January anyone can remember. I left home at lunchtime in the middle of yet another biblical deluge, but somewhere between Strensham Services and Bristol a stiff southwesterly started to tear great holes in the dirty, grey cloud blanket, the constant curtain of spray kicked up by the juggernauts thinned, then disappeared, until now I'm driving straight into a low winter sun.

With the clearing of the skies come the birds. Through the wet West Midlands I saw nothing more than a handful of magpies, jackdaws and rooks, a few distant and unidentifiable gulls, and a couple of kestrels – once the default raptor of our motorways but now an increasingly irregular sight. The second of them, a bedraggled male hunched on an overhanging light gantry near Worcester, seemed to encapsulate the gloom that surrounds this species' status in modern Britain, not to mention my own struggle to shake off the inevitable post-Christmas torpor.

Now, however, as I approach Taunton, everything changes. Sheep pastures are spackled with straggly flocks of winter thrushes, woodpigeons and stock doves that arrow purposefully across the six lanes; finches and tits skip from bush to bush as though blown by the backwash of trucks, and buzzards flap ponderously from dead trees and fence posts. When these ubiquitous raptors find a thermal, conjured by the late-afternoon sun, they're suddenly transformed into the scaled-down eagles they are, climbing gracefully and methodically as they use the last hour of daylight to proclaim their ownership of the sodden fields and pastures.

After two and a half hours behind the wheel, I'm ready for a break, and when a group of twenty or so starlings skims over the road I'm reminded that the Somerset Levels are among the best places in Britain to see their murmurations, the extraordinary pre-roost gatherings in which thousands upon thousands of birds perform a mind-meld of enormous proportions, each one seemingly surrendering its consciousness to a swirling, pulsating whole. Surely it's worth an hour's wandering around the lanes in search of them? Certainly it's more appealing than weak tea and ludicrously expensive cheese toasties at the fast-approaching services. I indicate left and let the 500 yards of the slip road take me into another country.

I should explain. Since the age of seven or eight, I've been a member of that much-maligned and even more misunderstood tribe – birdwatchers. Not a twitcher, you understand, the term trotted out disparagingly by the national press on the rare occasions that the world of ornithology intrudes upon their pages. Not for me midnight dashes up the motorway to catch a ferry to some bleakly beautiful Scottish island in the hope of seeing a tiny transatlantic stray that an autumn storm has thrown helplessly into our hemisphere, or teeth-chattering vigils on east coast headlands waiting to see what the winds will bring out of Siberia. No, a birdwatcher, plain and simple.

This is going to sound like stating the obvious, but a birdwatcher watches birds. They might, if they are one of those aforementioned twitchers, also tick species off a list (or more likely several lists); hence their alternative name of listers. They'll probably compare their hauls with like-minded individuals across the country, across the globe even. They can, if they happen to work for a conservation organisation such as the RSPB, British Trust for Ornithology or The Wildlife Trusts, or if they're one of the thousands of volunteers who make these and many smaller ornithological societies and clubs tick, turn their observations into hard science that, in the past at least, has helped shape environmental policies for governments of all stripes. Increasingly, they might squint down the barrel of a digital camera the same way the pioneering naturalists of the nineteenth century sighted their own ornithological finds down the barrel of a gun. Birds that, a hundred years ago, would have found themselves gathering dust in the glass cases of county museums, live on, bright-eyed and with every feather detail picked out in thousands of megapixels, on countless blogs and websites. But a birdwatcher watches birds. For many of us – most of us, probably – that's enough.

My own enthusiasm was fired from pretty meagre kindling – a primary school project, of which my only real memory is creating a collage picture of a then-rare osprey (little suspecting that thirty years later they'd be nesting only a few miles from that school), my mother's fondness for feeding garden birds, and occasional sightings of something unfamiliar during annual summer holidays at my nan's house in South Wales. These included a strange black and white creature, seemingly carrying a carrot in its bill, which scudded low over the beach at Rest Bay one overcast August day, which a nearby pub sign revealed to be an oystercatcher, starting my enduring fascination with wading birds.

And there were books, of course. I read anything and everything I could get my hands on, as this new obsession replaced my previous fascination with dinosaurs. No bird had quite the same capacity to induce awe and terror as a Tyrannosaurus rex, of course, but I suppose my eight-year-old self made the not unreasonable assumption that any of them, even colourful rarities like the golden oriole, were far more likely to turn up in the suburban East Midlands than the 'terrible lizard' itself.

The local library provided *The Observer's Book of Birds*, while birthdays delivered the RSPB's own similar effort, along with a much heavier tome that would never, these days, get away with calling itself a field guide. Quite apart from its doorstop size, the species accounts were brief and vague, and the drawings of a distinctly impressionistic bent. There's nothing wrong with reducing a rare passerine to a few bold pencil strokes, and these days I'd probably enjoy the same artwork in an exhibition, but to a young birdwatcher the illustrations only induced bafflement.

Finally, there was the *Reader's Digest Field Guide to the Birds of Britain*, which would also struggle to be considered portable with its slightly odd, letterbox shape, but which mixed wonderful artwork with precise descriptions and concise but fascinating little digressions into the folklore and cultural significance of the different species. It, or at least a later version of it, is sitting there in my birding rucksack even now.

Passionate as I was about birds, it's fair to say I was never of a very scientific turn of mind. Prior to going to secondary school, I'd heard all the scare stories from older kids about having to dissect rats and God knows what else in biology lessons, and being somewhat squeamish I dreaded it. Once I got there, however, biology sprang two genuine surprises. The first was a pleasant one, namely that dissection wasn't on the curriculum at all, and that I thoroughly enjoyed the subject. The second, a far more disappointing turn-up for the books, was that I didn't actually understand a great deal of it. So, my birdwatching remained strictly un-academic, and if you'd asked me at the time I'd have struggled to tell you anything about why I enjoyed it. The truth, of course, is that it's taken me until now to even begin to understand that.

Once caught, the birdwatching bug is never quite thrown off. Even during those periods of your life when you think it's taken a back seat, you still find yourself gazing into the middle distance as you talk to someone in the street, while struggling to make out if that really was a grey wagtail scurrying across the car park, rather than the more familiar pied.

So it was with me. By the time I went to university other interests (primarily that great British hobby 'going to the pub', plus music and cricket) had come along, but they never wholly took over. And then, in my mid-twenties, living in Cardiff, working as a newspaper subeditor and suffering with a chronic back condition, I found myself walking miles each day at the recommendation of my doctor. As lovely as Llandaff and Pontcanna Fields are, they can get a bit samey when seen every day for a month, and so I started taking a pair of binoculars along to see what birds I could find. And that was it. I was a birdwatcher once again, and this time there was no going back.

That's why I find myself standing at the roadside at East Lyng on a Friday afternoon in January. My journey to Cornwall is in connection with my job as editor of *Bird Watching* magazine. As you might imagine, managing to combine that childhood love of birds with the unfortunate adult need to earn a living is something of a dream job, and if, like any area of journalism, it contains its fair share of mundanity, it also contains more than its portion of unalloyed joy, not least in providing a cast-iron excuse for hanging around for large parts of every month while aiming my Swarovskis in the direction of feathered fly-pasts.

This particular stretch of road, as it happens, is one I know well. Any student of English history feels a sudden pang of recognition when, in East Lyng, they pass the signpost to Athelney. There, in January of 878, King Alfred of Wessex took refuge from the Danes among the marshes and thickets of the Levels, after the invading army fell upon his court at Chippenham and dispersed his household forces. The exploits that would earn him the epithet 'The Great' were still a few months away, and when he wasn't overcooking some unfortunate housewife's breadcakes you'd imagine he probably didn't have a great deal to do beyond watching the birds that thronged what was then a wetland wilderness. Although he probably ate a fair few of them too, and not just the wildfowl that still turn up on our own menus. Godwit, for example, from the Anglo-Saxon for 'good thing', is merely one modern bird name that reveals the species' past as a culinary delicacy, and a remarkable number of our native species remained on the menu to within living memory. In the terrible post-war winter of 1947, for example, even the likes of house sparrows were still being trapped to provide a mouthful or two of sustenance.

But I'm digressing. As I leave the village to the east, there are barriers across the road just beyond the last house, and signs warning of floods, but the way's still passable on foot for at least half a mile. The straight stretch of the A361 towards Burrow Mump (little more than a pimple in the grand scheme of things, but a veritable mountain in these parts) has been turned into a causeway, with the fields on both sides submerged. Close to the Alfred monument itself, on the low hill that is the original Isle of Athelney, water pours down the gentle slope and pools beyond the hedge.

Now it's fair to say that were I living in this locality I'd probably find the floods less than fascinating. If they're in your front garden – worse, in your front room – they cease to be a novelty, a magnificent force of nature, or a once-in-a-lifetime sight, and become a nuisance, a health hazard and a heartbreaking reminder of climate change, government incompetence or the refusal to listen to the wisdom of tradition (take your pick).

But I'm passing through, and selfishly find myself enjoying the sheer strange grandeur of what's before me. The immense lake to the north is criss-crossed by hedges and fences and studded with occasional trees, giving it an appearance that, you suspect, gets rather close to what Alfred himself might have seen. Back then, the Levels would have been an almost trackless, convoluted tangle of streams and dark meres, with willow thickets and alder carr clinging to the islets rising from the murk – not the semi-tamed arable land we see today. The landscape is simultaneously expansive, with the whole sky suddenly pouring itself into a pool between two hedges, and restrictive, oppressive even. You can well understand why even Guthrum and his fierce heathen warriors would have hesitated at the thought of following Alfred into this wilderness. Ravens, perhaps, might have found enough to sustain them in the form of unfortunate people and animals fallen foul of the waters, but those marching under the raven banner would have found things a good deal less hospitable.

But the long-ago struggles of a fugitive king are soon exiled to the far reaches of my mind. And it is the birds that do the banishing. No sooner have I started walking east along the road than I stop at a sign of movement to the right. There's a patch of land, maybe half of a small field, still above water, in the shadow of the raised causeway between East Lyng and Athelney; and as I focus the binoculars on it, I can see that it's alive with fieldfares and redwings – thrushes that pour across the North Sea to these islands from Scandinavia every winter. Such gatherings are common enough across the UK, but I've never seen them flocking quite so densely. Whatever the problems caused by the floodwaters, they seem to be turning the conditions to their advantage, feeding quickly and constantly, pulling worms and other goodies from the soft ground. Every now and then the last couple of ranks in the fieldfare flock leapfrog to the front, and so the gathering moves slowly eastwards with me, utterly heedless of my presence and intent only on making the best use of what little light is left to them.

To the north, little flurries of jackdaws and rooks lift from the fields beyond the trees, and two carrion crows harangue a buzzard as it sits in silent and unmoving vigil on a dead branch. Impressive as the raptor is in terms of size, it has to take a back seat to the marsh harrier that appears from the east, gliding low with long wings held in a shallow V, tethered tight to its own reflection. Its presence provokes consternation but not alarm among the mallards, teal and moorhens dabbling in the shallower areas – they move purposefully but unhurriedly towards the nearest cover, like office workers who, on hearing a genuine fire alarm for the first time, carry out the drill they've rehearsed a dozen times.

The sounds are as impressive as the sights. There's the whistling of wigeon from somewhere out of sight, and lapwings skirl and swirl, low over the waters, before coming to rest on the long island formed by a field boundary. They bicker for the best positions, only occasionally forgetting their private rivalries to gang up on an intruding black-headed gull.

From above comes a distinctive, two-note piping, a sound that speaks to any birder of wild, wide-open places. Craning my neck to look skyward, it takes me a good thirty seconds to find its source, even though I know what it will be. A loose group of around two hundred golden plovers flash and spangle in the last of the sun, performing their strange alchemy with every turn. At first they're dark, indistinct dots, before, banking left, they brighten into little white-hot ingots, finally turning again and falling as a rain of gold pieces.

All of this has me, for a moment, quite forgetting where I am. This sort of sight, with huge numbers of birds clinging to every square foot of dry land, every one of them intent only on its own survival, and seemingly completely oblivious to human presence, feels more like one of the world's great wetlands – Australia's Kakadu, maybe, or Brazil's Pantanal – than the fenlands of south-west England. I've been lucky enough, as part of my job, to visit such places, but this feels every bit as extraordinary.

No, more so, perhaps. For a good ten minutes I am quite literally entranced, unable to break my gaze away from this astonishing spectacle. Sporadic glimpses of lapwings' crests above the long grass just add to the exotic feel. Seen at a distance, they're chunky, pied creatures which only finally make a lasting impression when they take to the air, tumbling and falling while making a noise not unlike someone trying to tune in an old-fashioned radio. But seen close up, with the iridescent purples and greens of their backs glorious in the sunlight, and their jaunty crests visible, they're a sudden glimpse of far-off savannahs. 'So crowned cranes stalk Kenyan grass' writes the English poet Alison Brackenbury of them in the poem 'Lapwings', from her recent collection *Then,* and she's right. Perhaps somewhere deep down their appeal to us is that they rekindle buried memories of our own origins in a warmer, wider continent.

When finally I do drag my gaze away from them, I realise that behind the sounds of the gathered birds, the motorway has been keeping up its distant roar, trains have been clattering past on the way to Exeter and Plymouth, Land Rovers have been splashing through the little lake that's spreading onto the main road, and dog-walkers have been taking advantage of the lack of traffic to let their animals off the leash.

This whole extraordinary circus of avian life has been happening just yards away from all the paraphernalia of the modern world. The birds, in their way, have learned to live with it, even to take advantage of it, where they can. For all that we (quite rightly) blame ourselves for the decline of many species, we're also the reason why many of them are there in the first place.

Take the skylark, a species beloved of poets for its song and, until recently, emblematic of the downlands and open country of lowland Britain. In recent years it has undergone a worrying decline, with farming practices among the reasons blamed, but it would never have been so widespread and ubiquitous in these islands in the first place if man hadn't cleared the forests to allow sheep and cattle to graze.

Or the house sparrow, another bird that has suffered a huge drop in numbers and range in the last couple of decades. Again, our changing agricultural methods, along with modern building technology and the fashion for tidy gardens covered in decking, are blamed for what has happened, but the bird's very name suggests that it has long depended on the presence of man for both food and lodging. It must, of course, have originally managed without either, but thousands of years of living cheek by jowl have forged a complicated symbiotic relationship.

We Britons are proud of our tendency to self-deprecation. We're suspicious of anyone and anything that proclaims its virtues, its presence even, too loudly, and this attitude extends into the world of birdwatching. On the one hand that's down to necessity. We don't have the plethora of brightly coloured, sharply plumaged birds that you find in the tropics or around the Mediterranean; so if you're going to make a habit of watching birds in the British Isles, you'd better be able to get excited at the sight of what are rather disparagingly referred to as LBJs – Little Brown Jobs.

But standing here, watching the birds swarming across every inch of the Levels that's still above water, it occurs to me that we take the same view of birds as a whole, not just the individual creatures. We see them in our gardens, or on a walk in the country, we feed them and make notes on them, photograph and paint them. Some of us even write poems about them.

Only rarely, though, do we consider birds en masse. A great many experienced birdwatchers will tell you that Britain has little to compare with the great spectacles of the bird world. We have no large-scale migration bottlenecks to compare with Falsterbo in Sweden, or Tarifa in Spain. We have no massive gatherings of majestic cranes, such as you might see in Israel's Hula Valley, or in central Europe. There are no opportunities to watch noisy crowds of gaudy, bickering parrots, as at the clay-licks of Central and South America. And what do we have as an equivalent of the crack-of-dawn explosions of colour that are the cock-of-the-rock leks of Ecuador, or Peru?

Away to the north, just about where I know the M5 must be, a little cloud of black specks is starting to form, growing almost imperceptibly with every twist and turn. For a minute or two, it struggles to take shape, threatens to fall apart under the multiplicity of different instincts and urges contained within, then suddenly attains critical mass, a point at which every starling within sight decides that, if it's to make it through the coming night, it needs to be part of it.

And as I watch, a thought starts to take shape, hesitantly at first, but with growing conviction and confidence. *These* are our spectacles. What they might sometimes (and it is only sometimes) lack in colour, size and grandeur, they make up for by being all around us on these crowded islands as we go about our everyday lives. Often all that's required for us to see them, to be a part of them, is to stand still for a moment or two, and watch, and listen. Even when there's a bit more travel involved, or a longer wait, we're not talking about day-long treks into the back of beyond, or enduring terrible privations. These are wildlife spectacles that take place within our everyday world. That depend on being part of it, in some cases.

By the time I reach the car again, my decision is made. What does a year's worth of Britain's greatest bird spectacles look and sound like? I'm about to find out.

1   The Mating Game

It starts with a singleton, of course. A solitary bird, drifting on the edge of a loose group in midwinter. It's cold, and the days are short, so there's little time to spare from the constant struggle to find food, but when the sun breaks through the scattered cloud around midday, and briefly summons up enough strength to send steam rising from the puddles along the lakeside path, the chances are that the bird's thoughts turn to other things.

One other thing, to be exact. The propagation of its own genetic material, and so the survival of the species. When you're a bird facing umpteen natural and unnatural threats to your safety (and most do), as well as stiff competition for nesting sites and food, it does to think ahead.

In the case of this particular bird, a great crested grebe, pairing off is a process that happens every year. Not for it the sort of lifelong partnerships you get with some species, such as corvids. The aforementioned competition for nest sites contributes to the instability of pairs, with the parent birds often going their separate ways at just about the same time the young leave home in late summer. They *could* end up with the same partner the following year, of course – individual birds are always likely to return to both wintering and breeding sites that they know – but it's far from guaranteed.

And that's as far as it goes, for now. A thought, no more than that, as fleeting as the flock of long-tailed tits flitting through the nearby trees (in an example of the many and varied breeding strategies developed by birds, they will likely be a tight-knit family group). But it is a thought that will return with increasing frequency as the winter draws on. Our bird disappears beneath the dark, icy waters, back in pursuit of the fuel of life.

It's a couple of weeks later, and bitterly cold. There's a full moon jewelling the thick frost on the verges and tarmac all the way from Grantown-on-Spey. Early starts in the Scottish Highlands, even in late spring, can require layers of wool, fleece and Gore-Tex. In late January, that's doubly true.

Nobody's thinking about the temperature, though, and that's nothing to do with the noisy fan pumping heat into the hire car. Huddled beneath our beanie hats, all four of us are running and re-running half-a-dozen key ID characteristics through our minds, even though we know there's not much we could mistake for what we're seeking.

When we reach the sign welcoming us to Nethy Bridge, our silence deepens, and the tension tightens a notch or two further. We turn up through the village, into Abernethy Forest, and without being told each of us turns to stare into the pine-darkened reaches of the woods, two to each side of the car, which slows to little more than walking pace. Each time we reach an opening to one of the rides that criss-cross the forest, we stop for just long enough to satisfy ourselves that the dark shape in the middle of the track is only a fallen branch or, on one occasion, that the sudden flurry of movement is nothing more than a red squirrel.

Red squirrel! On any other day, seeing this elusive and charismatic native mammal would be reward enough for rising long before dawn and forgoing tea and porridge at the hotel. Long since forced from large parts of Britain by the bigger, North American grey squirrel, which carries diseases the reds are helpless against, and out-competes it for food, the red squirrel hangs on in good numbers in the mountain fastnesses of Scotland, thanks in part to the presence of pine martens, which can prey easily on the heavier greys, but which the lightweight reds can escape by climbing to the furthest, thinnest branches.

What we're looking for today has an even more tenuous grasp on survival in these islands. Capercaillies are our largest game birds by some distance, with an appearance that might be described as that of a black grouse on steroids, or even a rather more handsome version of a turkey. The name, from the Gaelic, means 'horse of the woods', and gives some impression of the size of the bird, and the noise it can make. The folk names of birds are often more interesting than the official moniker, but in this case the labels 'wood grouse' and 'heather cock' sell this striking bird very short.

Males are notoriously territorial, to the extent that they've been known to attack people and even Land Rovers, and this also means they're not overly fond of living in close proximity to their own kind. Combine a low population density with a preference for habitat that is relatively rare, and you have a recipe for slow but sure extinction.

In fact, capercaillies have already been extinct in Britain once, in the eighteenth century, the result of over-hunting and the clearance of large areas of forest, before being reintroduced in Scotland in the 1830s. This population prospered to the extent that the bird again became the target of shooters. In more recent decades, hunting has ended, but deer fences and over-grazing of the forest understorey have added to the pressure on the species. The pine marten, too, might not be helping – with no larger mammalian predators to keep them in the trees, as happens elsewhere in Europe where wolves and lynxes are present, they take the eggs of ground-nesting birds such as the 'caper'.

All this has added up to a worrying decline, from around 20,000 birds in the 1970s, to around 1,000 now. Conservation organisations are addressing the problem, but it's a touch-and-go situation.

But they're surviving in Scotland, at least. Sightings are hard to come by, especially on public land and the main reserves, and private estates are often the best places to look. But they're out there. Somewhere.

Today we're lucky. Sort of. A long odyssey through the forest, by road, track and narrow footpath, produces not a single male. We call in at the known lek sites – a lek being a sort of arena for the purposes of territorial posturing and sexual braggadocio – but to no effect. It will, admittedly, be easier to see them as the year draws on, yet this is still a disappointment.

But as we edge along one path around the perimeter of a little clearing, there's a sudden flurry of movement a few yards away, and a brown, mottled shape erupts into flight, scudding low over the bell heather and bilberry, until it reaches the denser cover of the pines. The rich chestnut edges to the tail mark it out as a female capercaillie. We're excited and relieved that at least some of the birds are around, knowing that where there are females, there should be males not too far away, and we resolve to come back another morning, soon.

To be a birdwatcher, of any level of enthusiasm or expertise, is to live your life according to a completely different calendar from the one you grew up with. Submitting to it is no easy task, though, because it brings with it small disappointments and unexpected melancholies that can daunt even the most indomitable heart.

There's the moment, for example, some time in June, when you notice the first couple of leggy, awkward wading birds picking their way around the shores of your nearest reservoir or gravel pit. Whatever excitement you might initially feel about finding black-tailed godwits, or maybe greenshanks, is quickly diluted then dissipated entirely by the realisation that these are adult birds, whose breeding attempts in the north of the UK, or on the Arctic tundra of Greenland or Norway or Svalbard, have failed. Maybe they were among the unlucky ones that didn't even manage to pair off in the first place. But whatever the reason for their presence, they're here because there's no time, in the brief summer of the far north, for second chances. Unable to fulfil one biological imperative – the perpetuation of their species – they've moved straight on to another, the urge to move south and get first choice of the prime feeding spots for the winter to come.

Because that's what we're talking about. With the summer solstice still a few days away, autumn migration will be already underway. The world is turning far faster than we might suspect, and birds are always several wingbeats ahead of us in realising that fact.

Journalists and other media types, admittedly, might find this slightly easier to deal with than most people, given that they're used to working months in advance. After all, Christmas comes in early September, in the world of monthly magazines.

But, for birdwatchers, this whole new timescale brings with it a corresponding consolation – or rather several. The first week of March, for example, can bring the first summer visitors to Britain into the south of these islands, with the frail, brown silhouettes of sand martins battling their way through the blustery winds like so many leaves left over from last autumn's bonfires.

Even before that, there are the first signs of new life. Right now, in the middle of this spirit-crushing second half of January, with the weather at its worst, the days stubbornly refusing to get longer, and the festive celebrations a dim memory, birds are getting ahead of the game. The indomitable robin, undaunted by winter or darkness, turns its song up a notch or two and pours its silvered notes into the cold air. Blue tits and chaffinches dart in and out of nest holes and boxes, bidding to secure the most desirable residences for raising a family. Grey herons' nests clot the top branches of bare trees, and in quarries and crags ravens return to nest sites that have been their homes since the days in which they were gods, or at least the earthly messengers of the divine. And across certain areas of Scotland, the Pennines of northern England, and the hills of North Wales, black grouse are heading to their own leks with a single, unshakeable purpose.

In many cases, black grouse will have started returning to their leks in November, or even earlier. While the females only make their appearance at these sites (and black grouse are very faithful to the same leks year after year) around the beginning of March, the males gather much earlier. That's why, just a week or so after my failed 'caper' quest, I find myself in a hide looking out across Welsh moorland just before dawn. The weather – cold and crisp – is perfect, and the habitat looks just right, with forest nearby, and a scattering of individual trees intruding onto the moor.

Dawn comes slowly on a day of scudding cloud, and it takes a good twenty minutes for a succession of impressionistic pencil marks to become the fence lines of a sheep enclosure, for a shadow to become a low shrub, and for a little jungle of bushes to become the birds we came seeking, a slight rise in the temperature seeming to suddenly thaw them from their stationary vigil.

Each of half-a-dozen huddles of undergrowth gradually resolves itself into a male black grouse – or blackcock, to give them their old name – as our binoculars and scopes do their work, taking in the largely purple-black body, with white wing flashes, the lyre-shaped tail trailing behind, and the shockingly red wattles, the only real points of colour in a landscape still struggling to cope with the idea of day.

While capercaillie leks may involve a solitary male – especially these days with the population in decline – black grouse can be found in much larger numbers. In some parts of eastern Europe leks can attract more than 150 males. In the UK, a group of thirty would be considered pretty exceptional, twenty would be good, and the six we can see (within minutes two more bushes transform before our eyes) make up a more than respectable count. As we're about to find out, even eight black grouse can put on quite a show.

We hear them announce the beginning of their strange ritual. The flight call of one of their close relatives, the red grouse, coming from somewhere close at hand, seems to set them off, and all at once our amorous adventurers are strutting back and forth, uttering their own low, liquid display call, and presumably eyeing their rivals nervously. The tails are cocked and spread wide and white, making it appear as though snow has suddenly gathered in the hollows and cwms of the little plateau, while the wattles flare brighter than ever. And once or twice a bird jumps up, briefly, onto one of the fence posts, the better to survey the scene of his planned future triumph, before returning to the ground and joining the others in their patient wait for the smaller, greyer females. It might be two months yet before the greyhens arrive, but the males will be back here day after day, displaying with greater and greater fervour, until all that bubbling and squeaking becomes a crouching, creeping parade punctuated with mock and occasionally real fights, in an attempt to gain the best positions in the lek, usually those closest to the centre. As a bird grows older, it generally has more chance of attaining this coveted spot. When you're a black grouse, experience counts for everything.

If the spectacle lacks the brilliant colour that you get with similar birds abroad, such as the two cock-of-the-rock species in South America, or the Raggiana birds-of-paradise in New Guinea, it's all the more impressive for being so open. There's no craning the neck to look into treetops, or around massive tree trunks, where black grouse are concerned.

For six months, then, this lek could be the focus of their every waking moment, and once the females arrive things really gather pace. Males dash to and fro to meet multiple opponents, and although full-blooded fights don't always result, the movement and the noise can be astonishing, with their 'rook-oo' call carrying loud and clear across the moors.

Female black grouse, it's fair to say, don't necessarily go for the nice guys. Fighting often seems to attract them, as does mating, to the extent that they'll often rush to a male who has just copulated with another female. Some males, every year, will miss out, and all that effort will come to nothing. Once it's over, the males have nothing to do with the nesting, incubation and feeding of the young, so presumably they have plenty of time to reflect on their experiences and vow to do better next time around.

Today, that's in the future. Our grouse are content to stake out the arena of their showdowns to come, pacing back and forth carefully and measuring their opponents' worth, perhaps, in the brightness of their wattles, the whiteness of their undertails, the harsh resonance of their calls, all the time calculating if they'll be among the winners in March and April. In one respect, at least, black grouse are like birdwatchers, forced to think months ahead all the time.

Back home in Leicestershire, the only hint that spring is little more than a month away is given by the ravens up at the nearby quarry, who are already back at their sprawling nest, adding twigs to repair the damage caused by winter winds. It's cold, and snow is forecast, but they might have laid eggs already. It will be a hard struggle, if so, but there's no more resourceful bird than this biggest of British crows; and there are few birds I enjoy seeing more.

I make my way down towards the village, pausing at the little viewpoint to look across to a low, blue shadow on the western horizon. Cannock Chase. Incredible as it seems now, capercaillies were reintroduced there in the 1950s. The thought of such huge, conspicuous game birds parading around just beyond the edge of the West Midlands conurbation seems utterly ridiculous, but every now and then I'll meet an older local birder who can remember being taken to see them as a child. For a minute or two, I imagine them lekking somewhere beneath where Rugeley power station's cloud plume is currently flowering. At some stage, presumably, there must have been a single remaining male, doing his thing for fewer and fewer females, and then none, and then silence.

Oppressed a little by this thought, I make my way along what used to be a railway track but is now a footpath hemmed in by trees and hedges, leading to the leisure centre. Beyond a playing field, I have the choice to turn right, across a little stream and back past the cemetery to my house, or left, to walk round the little fishing lake behind the local leisure centre.

When I was a child, this latter was little more than a large, muddy puddle, part of one of the many open-cast mines or brickworks that dotted the area. When the area was eventually landscaped to form part of the leisure-centre grounds, they deepened the lake, made the banks a bit more solid, and stuck an artificial island, soon garlanded by trees, in the middle.

Wherever you go in the world, water attracts birds of all types. Waterbirds especially, of course, and it wasn't long before the lake had its own population of mallards and Canada geese, utterly used to humankind and more than willing to beg for bread and other scraps from whoever came near. The geese, in fact, can be pretty aggressive when they want to be.

Then, around 1997, when I was twenty-seven, and a year or so after I'd been born again as a birdwatcher, I was walking round the banks of this little lake while on a weekend visit back to the old town. The geese tried their luck, barring my way in a transparent attempt to extort bread, only backing off, with a hiss, at the last moment. Mallards splashed around doing what mallards do, which involves a distinctly Neanderthal approach to courtship (the unfortunate females are sometimes drowned during these distressingly violent episodes). But out on the lake, just at the far end of the island, something quite different was happening.

Two birds glided gracefully and silently through the water, one a little ahead of the other. Just a little smaller than the mallards, dark-bodied, and with long, elegant necks that instantly set them apart from any of the ducks. I walked towards them, and before I got much closer I could see an even more obvious distinguishing feature. The white face of each bird was topped by black, backswept plumes that they occasionally raised and fanned a little, but which were generally left flat to ruffle a little in the wind, while the finishing touch was the chestnut and black 'tippets' that irresistibly called to mind Elizabethan gentlemen, or the elaborate costume of some medieval clergyman.

Great crested grebes. Because they were pictured in the opening pages of my field guide, I was absolutely familiar with how they looked, but while I'd seen them a few times before, way out in the middle of reservoirs usually, I was utterly unprepared to find them here.

This was more due to the long hiatus in my birding career than the bird's actual level of rarity, or rather lack of it. Great crested grebes, you see, had quietly been staging one of British ornithology's great comebacks. In the Victorian era, they were slaughtered in their tens of thousands for the plumage trade, with a predictably catastrophic effect on numbers. Fortunately, before it was too late, this largest of the western hemisphere's grebes (a family of highly specialised diving birds) became the focus of what might be the most successful conservation campaign of all time.

That might sound like an extravagant claim, given that there are still only six thousand or so pairs in the UK. But the successful efforts of a group of mainly well-to-do ladies to save this beautiful creature were to lead to something bigger than they could possibly have imagined. The Royal Society for the Protection of Birds was born out of it, and not much more than a century later the RSPB boasts over 1.1 million members. Large areas of the UK are owned and managed by the charity, with all wildlife, not just birds, in mind; its reserves attract new generations of birdwatchers to take up the hobby and the cause; and its members are ignored by politicians at their peril.

Six thousand pairs isn't an immense amount, but great crested grebes are never going to be as numerous as, say, mallards. Each pair needs a significant amount of water to provide food for them and their young, and they like their own space. They're widespread, rather than numerous, but that means that most people in the UK live within easy reach of places where they can be found.

Significantly, in the last few decades, they've spread into the sort of locations that, a century ago, no self-respecting great crested grebe would have even considered. Gravel pits and city centre park ponds are now just as likely to provide a home for these distinctly aristocratic-looking birds as the lakes of stately homes. That's partly due to population pressure – more birds surviving means that some will have to be a little less fussy about their habitat than in the past. But it's also, perhaps, a small tribute to the conservation-minded British public. Old industrial sites and purely utilitarian stretches of water are, more often than previously, allowed to develop a certain amount of 'wildness'. While we could still do a lot better on this count, in the case of the great crested grebe the little we have done brings with it a great bonus for the birdwatcher.

In winter, the grebes retain their sleek, elegant lines, but that collar-cum-mantle and the extraordinary tufts are nowhere to be seen. The birds occasionally gather in good numbers at such times, especially at sites such as Rutland Water, but by early spring they're back at their breeding sites.

They have particular requirements for these. Water up to five metres deep, and at least a hectare of open water per pair, while vegetation around the banks is tolerated as long as the waters aren't too narrow. The nest is a heap of aquatic vegetation, the majority of it underwater, floating and occasionally tethered to a branch or trunk, and although it'll be concealed in reeds where possible, on occasion it will be worryingly open and vulnerable.

The leisure-centre lake, unglamorous as it was, fulfilled all those criteria. First one, then another bird, must have come across it and deemed it suitable, and the pair I saw were probably fairly recent colonists. But life is instantly easier for the birds at such a site than at a large reservoir. The lake's only big enough for one pair, and its small size means that it would take some finding in the first place, so the male has the luxury of facing no immediate competition. Female grebes, like the females of most bird species, can be fussy nonetheless. They have to be. They need to know that they're choosing a mate that will pass on good genes, and that will help them to perpetuate their own genes.

In many species this might be done by assessing the brightness and colour of the male's plumage. In others it might be by taking note of the relative size of certain parts of the plumage – in swallows, for example, males with longer tail streamers do better in the reproductive stakes, even though the streamers are a hindrance to them in the business of flying and catching insects. Known as the handicap principle, this works by the female seeing that the males with the longest tails can afford the energy and effort needed to manage such appendages.

Now, it might be a lie to say that female great crested grebes care nothing for appearances, because both sexes have a handsomeness that borders on the foppish, but when it really comes down to it what she's looking for is a good dancer. So, for that matter, is the male – everything about this species' courtship rituals is based around a perfect symmetry that's unusual in the bird world.

As I watched, back in 1997, the pair started affirming their interest in each other by swimming face to face just a few inches apart and, ironically enough, shaking their heads. After some of the shakes, they swept their long bills elegantly through the feathers of their wings and back, as if pointing out to their potential mate the luxuriance of their plumage, or threw their heads back; throughout, their collars were puffed out into genuine ruffs. They might have been going through these moves for a few days already, weeks even, and it's the most frequently seen part of this bird's repertoire of courtship rituals.

What follows generally needs a bit of luck or a lot of persistence to see. I turned away from the lake a moment to look for the source of an unfamiliar contact call, and by the time I looked back only one bird was left. Or was it? The water in front of it rippled with disturbance, and the second grebe suddenly emerged in an upright posture that reminded me of nothing so much as a penguin, before pirouetting right in front of the other bird's face. That's a pretty neat trick, especially when you're used to seeing the far less sophisticated approach of mallards, but it's nothing to what came next.

The birds parted, and headed for the area around the island, disappearing beneath the water in turn. I amused myself by trying to guess where each would break the surface next, but tired of it, and started preparing to move on.

Then they were both visible again, maybe thirty yards apart. The clean lines of their heads and bills were marred somewhat by the tangle of green, dripping weed that each had pulled out from the lake-bottom, but grebes know how to turn an unpromising prop to their advantage. They turned towards each other and started swimming at considerable speed.

Just as it appeared a collision was inevitable, each of them rose into a sharply vertical posture, white breast to white breast, presenting the underwater vegetation to the other with the eternal optimism of the hopeful lover.

I know. Anthropomorphism is a sin, but it's hard to resist when it comes to great crested grebes. Maybe it's the very concept of birds dancing, the pavane-like nature of their processional courtship curiously appropriate to their Elizabethan appearance. Or maybe it's the fact that, as previously mentioned, both male and female have to make an effort, and that appeals to us in these enlightened times. Being able to see a performance such as theirs on the most unpromising of waterholes just adds to its beauty and sheer strangeness. Out in the wilds you come to expect that sort of thing. Confronted with it round the back of a corrugated steel leisure centre and two small business parks, on a drizzly Wednesday morning, you can be briefly convinced that all the luck in the world is running your way.

Finally, there's a second great pleasure that comes from finding that great crested grebes are nesting on your local lake. It would be pushing it a little to call it spectacular, as such, but it very definitely scores highly on the cute-o-meter (and don't believe even the most steely-eyed twitcher when they say that they don't do cute). The baby grebes, when they hatch, are tiny, fuzzy, black-and-white striped creatures, which resemble nothing quite so much as a mint humbug that's been left in a coat pocket too long and has picked up all the fluff of a dozen tumble-dryers. And if that isn't enough to reduce you to a bleary-eyed, cooing lump of jelly, their handsome parents also have the endearing habit of swimming around with the photogenic youngsters nestling on their backs. Grebes are the gift that just keeps on giving.

If birdwatching instantly teaches us something about time, the seasons and the artificiality of man's calendar, it quickly follows that up by convincing us that everything we know about geography is wrong. Britain, we're always being told, is a small island; however, while it's true we have neither the area nor the extreme variation in habitat of, say, the United States, we have more than enough to spring surprise after surprise. When I started work at *Bird Watching* magazine, for example, in an office block perched on the edge of the Cambridgeshire Fens, I was astonished to find that marsh harriers, a bird that I've seen only once at home, less than fifty miles away, were ten a penny there.

Nowhere did such diversity of habitat become more obvious than on my first winter trip to northern Scotland. We spent a day birdwatching along the Moray coast, between Inverness and Lossiemouth, and despite fierce, stingingly cold winds, saw all manner of wonderful birds. There were sleek divers of all shapes and sizes, riding low in the water and butting the waves like the battle fleets that once steamed out of Invergordon. Fire-eyed Slavonian grebes, subtly beautiful and mysterious even in their non-breeding plumage. Great rafts of eiders, their rather clumsy, clunky appearance completely at odds with the image of supreme softness their name instantly conjures. Gannets wheeling and diving at the far edge of sight. I drank in the experience of finally seeing, in the flesh, page after page of my field guide brought to life, pages that I'd never needed in my Midlands hometown.

As the light started to fade, we stared down our scopes into the wide expanse of Findhorn Bay, its mudflats twinkling yellow then white as a dense mass of golden plovers turned away from the wind. Other waders picked their way around the water's edge, a few pintails swam in the shallows, and gulls loafed, as gulls do. It was a good way to end a great day, but the excitement wasn't yet over, or at least not for our guide, Alex.

He began to make the sort of noises that birdwatchers do when something really exciting comes along. A sort of low-frequency muttering, accompanied by increasingly frantic movements of his binoculars and scope. I and the other two birdwatchers with us tensed, wondering which rarity was going to be announced to us imminently. King eider? Brünnich's guillemot? Maybe even a white-billed diver?

'Got it!' said Alex, glancing up at us with a look of quiet triumph. The tension was unbearable, but the silence remained unbroken. I decided to take matters into my own hands, and put my eye to the scope.

There, picked out in all the gloriously crisp, sharp detail that the best Austrian optics can provide, was a single great crested grebe. Its plainer winter plumage did it no favours, and for a moment I was wondering just what else had sparked Alex's excitement. And then I understood. Up here, the grebes are scarce enough to qualify as a great bonus tick to round off a highly productive day.

The incident set me thinking about the whole concept of ticking off lists of the birds we see, but mainly about how what we think of as Britain's birding landscape is in reality a mosaic of different habitats and eco-systems, inextricably linked and ever-changing, yet separate and distinct at the same time. It could, conceivably, leave you dispirited at how you'll ever get to grips with the variety of wildlife that's out there. Or – and I can't recommend this highly enough – it could convince you that getting to know your own little corner of the world inside out is a worthy aspiration for any naturalist, and one that will take you at least a lifetime to fulfil.

Bowing with the Beautiful

I dream of birds. Sometimes, the experience is so vivid that I wake excited at the myriad new and strange species I've seen, only to face disappointment, moments later, when realising they were merely a strange trick of the memory.

That said, it has occurred to me that I could always keep a list of the birds I've seen purely in dreams. The most memorable, I think, were the flock of half-a-dozen black wheatears – a gorgeously dapper species found in the Iberian peninsula – that turned up in a back garden similar, but not identical, to my parents'. The unlikeliness of such an encounter made no impression on my subconscious. Neither did the subsequent appearance, in the same garden, of a full-sized polar bear. I finally woke with a start, and with the melancholy feeling that a great sighting had escaped me.

But a different type of bird dream comes to me, too. It can start in February, on still, windless nights, but it really makes itself known in April, when warmer temperatures make sleeping with the window open possible, or even necessary.

It can start when sunrise is still little more than an idea. Somewhere in the east, the sky's lowest fringes are just beginning to bleach out, although you'd be hard pressed to tell if that was down to the coming sun, or the sodium glow of the cities of the East Midlands.

A thin, silvery voice speaks to my sleeping self of forests and rivers, of heath and hedgerow, of park and garden and the unloved, unlooked-for spaces that punctuate our everyday lives. I hear it and straight away I'm wondering, and wandering in search of its source. I know the voice belongs to a bird, striking up its song, but I know nothing of what it is, or what it's trying to say to me. I only know that it has the beauty distinctive to anything that is utterly and indefatigably itself, and that I want to hear it more loudly and clearly, and see the singer.

But the instant I move off after it, there's another voice, and another, similar yet distinctive, and then finally another altogether, a stronger, more confident, but melodious and soft voice. It's as if this voice is speaking a different language to the first, although perhaps one that shares a common origin. Welsh to the former's Breton, perhaps. And then it too is joined by another similar voice, and another, and all the voices heard so far are raised a notch higher as a fifth, sixth, seventh and seventeenth song-language join the babel of tongues battling to be heard.

The dream-me who hears all this eventually gives in to the inevitable, and lets the torrent of song wash over and through him. The song speaks of distances and journeys and of other voices heard along the way. It talks of renewal and rebirth. It is energising, and cleansing, and I open my eyes from the dream to realise it has become a part of my waking self, and that spring is once again sprung.

It's a dream you can have, too.

Most of us recognise a few bird songs, at least. The cuckoo's disyllabic public service announcement that spring has arrived. The tuneful, rhapsodic performance of the blackbird, from atop the TV aerial of your house. The silvery strands of the robin's broadcast, flung upon midwinter snows and balmy spring evenings alike. The suburban jangle of the chaffinch.

But there's more, so much more. The dawn chorus – that sudden outpouring of song to greet the coming of daylight – is found all over the world, but a lucky combination of factors makes Britain's chorus better than most. Than any, some would say.

For a start, we have four very distinct seasons, which means that mating and breeding are concentrated into a relatively short space of time. In warmer climes, these can go on for much longer. Here, in addition to establishing and maintaining a territory, songbirds have to attract a mate (or re-woo last year's) within the few short weeks that occur from late winter through to late spring. They can't afford to waste time, because in many cases the food that their nestlings need will only be available during a narrow window of opportunity; and they might also be hoping to raise more than one brood. Any delay risks them getting behind schedule, or even missing out on breeding altogether.

For another thing, we have a dawn chorus that builds gradually but steadily, from a single species singing in the middle of winter, to scores lifting their voices in spring, bolstered by the arrival of migrant songbirds – primarily but not exclusively warblers – from the southern hemisphere.

So, in the darkest days of winter, you'll hear little in the way of song. Birds still *call*, but that's completely different. A call is a way of alerting other birds to the presence of a predator (or to your own immediate presence) or, who knows, to the discovery of a food source. It's functional, and so is short and sharp and not necessarily sweet.

A song has another dimension entirely. It has a functional element, certainly – the singer is to some extent saying 'I'm here' as loudly as possible, in the hope of scaring off rivals and earning the admiration of a mate. But it's also saying 'I'm here' in a much more metaphysical sense, announcing to the world the singer's entire reason for being. Not for nothing are they called songbirds.

Robins are the first to break into song each morning, and perhaps this explains the lasting British affection for this species as much as their bright-red breasts and their confiding nature do. The male and female hold separate feeding territories at this time and both sing from the middle of winter; in other British species it's the male that does most if not all of it. Robins are, despite their somewhat cuddly reputation, extremely aggressive when they need to be – which is a lot of the time – and that sweet song is just one of the weapons in their armoury, used to try to ward off rivals.

Significantly, the midwinter song of the robin is a more understated, subdued and plaintive version of their spring symphony. The birds know it's serving a slightly different purpose, and they also know they don't have to be quite as loud – there are no other singers to compete with.

Most, if not all songbirds, also have a quieter, more muted version of their song, known as a subsong, which they use as a sort of warm-up for the main event. So, if you were to find the wintering grounds of, say, a UK-breeding blackcap, which lie south of the Sahara, you'd hear these sweet songsters tuning up for the breeding season ahead. And perhaps just before they leave for northern Europe you'd hear their subsong segue seamlessly into the full song, now perfected.

In the earliest days of spring, then, the dawn chorus can take some hearing. Subsongs are whispered from bushes and trees, and although there's a slowly gathering volume and intensity to the music it's got a long way to go before it reaches its full glory.

The trigger for the full performance, as with so many things in the world of birds, is a change in light levels, imperceptible to us but as obvious as a motorway sign to the singers. On a certain day in early spring – and it will vary according to the latitude you're at, as well as the local habitat and weather conditions – a song becomes a duet, becomes a chorus.

British birdwatchers are an affable, helpful lot, but you still get the occasional squabble between twitchers, questioning the authenticity of each other's lists or the validity of the latest sighting; and every now and then a row will break out over an alleged incidence of suppression, when a record of a particularly interesting bird is kept from the general birdwatching public by those in the know. The finders might have a good reason for this, such as wanting to protect a nest site, but it rarely happens without a dust-up.

Most of the time, though, to meet another birder in the hide, or on the path through your local reserve, is to be assured of a cheerful 'good morning', followed by a recitation of their most recent birdwatching triumphs and woes, and then detailed directions to the best birds nearby. Sometimes, they'll even accompany you, especially if the birds in question are at all rare, even at a local level. It's not unusual in the world of birding to find yourself making polite conversation with a stranger standing on some puddly, muddy cart-track miles from anywhere, waiting for an unobliging passage migrant to turn up and make everybody's day worthwhile. And therein lies something of a problem. Because, for many of us – most of us, even – birdwatching is essentially a solitary pursuit.

The reasons for this are many. It has something to do with the way that, while popular, it is not *that* popular. You could walk into any pub in the UK and reasonably expect to strike up a conversation about football, but fellow birders, and especially fellow birders of roughly equivalent interests and abilities, are rather thinner on the ground.

It has something to do with the image birdwatching has always had. Not out and out negative exactly, but definitely nerdy and slightly comical. Not many birdwatchers have been in a hurry to proclaim their love of the subject to the rest of the world.

But there's something else. Birdwatching, in some respects, is just a replacement activity for the hunting that we'd all have engaged in once. This is at its most obvious when you see full-on twitchers looking to 'bag' another tick, but an element of it is there with the most casual of birdwatchers, too. Getting a good look at even the commonest of birds means learning a certain amount of stalking and fieldcraft. In the same way as with the hunter, it pays to learn your quarry's habits and routines.

But more than that, part of the appeal of birdwatching for myself, and I suspect many people, is that it's a good cover for another activity generally derided by Britons – spending time on your own thinking about things. We're not, in Britain, overly given to self-reflection. We look with suspicion upon the willingness of Americans to go to psychiatrists. Meditation is still viewed by many as belonging to the exotic East. Philosophy is for the Greeks. Or is it the French? Birdwatching, along with that other great British outdoor pursuit – walking the dog – is as close as some of us get to being able to consider the big questions in life, to commune openly with something much larger than ourselves, without frightening the neighbours.

That was how it started, or restarted, for me. I've mentioned how, when I lived in Cardiff in my twenties, birdwatching gave me an incentive to get out on a long walk each day, with all the hoped-for benefits for my bad back, and the more I did it the more I rediscovered my love of birding. But the walking itself was important, too. It might sound obvious, but walking takes time, time that we're otherwise not inclined to give ourselves in the middle of our busy lives. I found myself thinking longer, and harder, about all sorts of things. I worked out what I wanted to do in my life, and where I wanted to be. I even started writing poetry, for heaven's sake.

Around five years ago I decided to do all my birdwatching for the following year on foot, with the intention of writing a feature for *Bird Watching* about it. While I wasn't a big twitcher or lister, I had nevertheless got into the habit of driving from one birdwatching site to another, within a twenty-mile radius of home.

Replacing that habit with a strictly pedestrian routine saved me an awful lot of petrol, helped me shed three stone in weight, and reminded me that walking, and birdwatching, can be therapy for a troubled, or simply tired, mind.

But the change of routine had an effect on my birding as well. As I walked between places I started to notice new things about the behaviour of even the most familiar species. I started to pay attention to the marginal, less obvious habitats in between the reserves and the parks and gardens and farmland. Above all, I started to realise just how much of birdwatching is actually bird-listening. And once learned, it's a lesson that enriches your birdwatching experience more than you could ever have dreamed.

It's early April, and I'm down at Gracedieu Woods, a mile or so from home. I carry out a woodland bird survey here once a month, so I'm planning to use this opportunity to 'get my ear in' ahead of a trip to one or two dawn chorus hotspots.

It's cold, and as I walk the first few yards into the trees, still dark. At least, it seems that way to me, but somewhere a bird has detected a thinning of the gloom and decided to salute it the only way it knows how. A robin, of course, spinning the silvery thread of its song out across the understorey of this deciduous wood, a remnant of the original Charnwood Forest.

I stand and listen. There are more robins, further in, and in no time at all blackbirds are joining in, with their strong but sweet, fluty tones. They effortlessly run through intricate variations on a theme, with an effect that's as close to what we recognise as music as any British bird achieves.

But if blackbirds are the classical musicians of the British scene, then song thrushes are the jazz improvisers. Their habit of singing short, distinctive phrases loudly, clearly and two or three times over has long been noted; Robert Browning's poem 'Home Thoughts from Abroad' highlights the quality:

> That's the wise thrush; he sings each song twice over,
> Lest you should think he never could recapture
> The first fine careless rapture.

There are two things to note at this point. One is that all the birds singing so far are species that rely, for the most part, on worms and other creatures of the forest floor for their food. These food sources can reasonably be expected to be around even now, when the sun is just a rumour beneath the eastern horizon. That old saying about 'the early bird catching the worm' is perfectly correct, and so our robins, blackbirds and song thrushes are setting out to establish territorial rights as early as possible, ahead of what could be a day of considerable friction between competing males.

The other point to note is that the singing of the song thrush generally increases in complexity as the season goes on, and as the years go by, because like all the best jazz musicians it has no qualms about appropriating a phrase here, a riff there, from other birds. And not just the birds in its immediate vicinity, either. I've stood outside my house on a warm May evening and listened to a song thrush on a leylandii repeating the two-note call of the curlew over and over. There are curlews a few miles away, but very few, so perhaps it picked up this neat trick when migrating curlew passed over; or perhaps the thrush spends its winters on one of our warmer coasts, where it's in close proximity to the large waders.

This habit of cutting and pasting the songs of other birds into your own is probably given its fullest expression by the marsh warbler. Like most of its family, it's a rather unprepossessing bird to look at – a Little Brown Job if ever there was one – and it's not easy to find in the UK, being confined mainly to Kent and parts of Worcestershire where it can find its preferred habitat of rank, seasonally flooded vegetation.

Whatever the marsh warbler lacks in looks, though, it makes up for with the ingenuity and virtuosity of its song. During his first year, on the breeding grounds in Europe and Asia, the wintering grounds in south-east Africa, and all points between, each male picks up the songs of around seventy-five other species, then splices them together into a single symphonic whole. Each song is different, of course, because no two birds will have heard exactly the same species, and intriguingly each male also sticks to what he first learned, with no extra snatches of song added after the first year. Every male is a living history of its own first year of life, compelled to tell you the same anecdotes about its travels over and over again.

The marsh warbler arrives in the UK late, compared to our other summer visitors. Sometimes it's June before it turns up, but the other members of this large family start to trickle in from mid-March. Some, indeed, stay here throughout the colder months, ekeing out a living. Dartford warblers do so in the dense gorse and brush of (mainly coastal) heaths, while Cetti's warbler, a recent colonist with an unmistakable, explosive song, skulks deep within reed beds and damp scrub. Blackcaps, on the other hand, have adapted to garden feeders to get through the cold months, while chiffchaffs hang around sewage works and farm buildings, especially in the south-west, looking for insects.

As I stumble a little further into the wood, one of the latter starts up with his insistent, two-note song, and is answered by yet another, further in. It's not so much a duet as a shoot-out, of course, and no other chiffchaffs yet feel inclined to argue the toss. Instead, there's a gathering cacophony of great tits – some of them using a two-note song not unlike the chiffchaff – and finch-song: the quiet, understated warbling of bullfinches, the light, metallic tinkling of goldfinches, the wheezing and twittering of greenfinches, and the descending jangle of the chaffinch.

Studies have shown that the chaffinch's song varies subtly from place to place, although not so much that a birder could necessarily tell the difference. These 'dialects', it's thought, serve the purpose of preventing inbreeding: female chaffinches learn to listen for a song significantly different from what they've heard from their fathers and male siblings.

By the time I've tried and failed to decide whether there's any difference between the songs of the chaffinches here and those at work, the sun is clear of the Charnwood hills, and the temperature is noticeably a few degrees warmer. The snap and crackle of twigs overhead betray the busy presence of grey squirrels, and the warm light filtering through the branches and budding leaves spotlights one, two, three and finally a loose crowd of small grey-brown birds perched on the edge of the small clearing, each ducking in and out of cover in turn.

Like a band in a studio overlaying old tracks on new to build up a single piece of music, we have the final layer of song.

Blackcaps chortle closest at hand, and a little further away, perhaps provoked by them, there's the very similar rippling, babbling song of the closely related garden warbler. For a moment it rivals the sweetness of the former's outpourings, but the irresolute ending, lacking the blackcap's emphatic flutiness, is like the unsatisfying fade-out of a radio edit of a great song, rather than the drums and power chord full-stop of the album version.

Soon willow warblers are joining in, too, their song like a sadder, thinner and more affecting version of the chaffinch's; and from away on the edge of the wood there's the excited, scratchy jibber-jabber of the whitethroat. It takes all these insect-eaters a while to join in, because they have to wait until their prey starts fluttering around to feed, but once they do they're impossible to ignore.

I listen for as long as my aching back and the pressing need to go to work will allow, then walk slowly home. If I was being churlish, I might reflect upon what I didn't hear – no redstart, or pied flycatcher, no 'spinning sixpence' song of the wood warbler. No purring turtle doves. No cuckoo, even, although I might at least hear one of them at Gracedieu before the spring is out.

But I'd also have heard a quite different but equally wonderful dawn chorus had I gone a couple of miles in any direction. Up on the more open spaces of Charnwood Forest, I could have expected yellowhammers jangling out their 'little bit of bread and no cheese' song from telephone wires, skylarks exulting from somewhere high above the heaths, and curlews delivering their ecstatic, bubbling trill as they glide over sheep pastures.

While the majority of passerines – that biological order of birds commonly, albeit somewhat inaccurately, known as songbirds – probably fall into the soprano bracket, contralto at deepest, there are even deeper 'songs' out there. The low, insistent throb of the bittern's 'boom', for a start, a bassline familiar to anyone living around the fenland and marshes of East Anglia and, thankfully, increasingly far-flung areas of the rest of the UK (a pair have bred at Attenborough, on the edge of Nottingham, as I write).

But wherever you are in the UK, whatever you're hearing, the phenomenon of the dawn chorus is extraordinary. Extraordinary in its range, its volume, in the way that each song seems to find its own space, its own frequency. And extraordinary in the fact that it will all happen again tomorrow, and tomorrow, until breeding is done for another year.

Having made the case for the glory of the dawn chorus, I'm bound to point out that birdsong in Britain can be wonderful at any time of day – it's just that you won't find quite the same intensity and range as you do at first light, when most of the male birds in these islands, along with a few of the females, are intent on announcing their continued existence, their health, vitality and virility, their possession of a desirable territory and/or residence, and their availability for intimate liaisons.

If there's another time in the day that does approach dawn as a good time to listen to birdsong, it's dusk. Many of the principles are the same – the birds are taking their last opportunity to send their aural CV out to prospective partners and rivals, before they settle down for the increasingly short night.

Blackbirds and song thrushes are particularly fond of indulging in a little twilight serenade, with the former also prone to greeting the approaching darkness with their persistent 'chink, chink' alarm call. Other small birds, such as blue tits, also sing late. And others, such as the grasshopper warbler, take centre stage at the dimming of the day, pouring out their strange, mechanical 'reeling' song (like a bicycle freewheeling or a fishing reel being played out) just as everything else is falling silent.

Other songs mainly heard at dusk and into the hours of darkness also tend to have similarly strange qualities – the vaguely mechanical 'churring' of nightjars, the corncrake's call, a recitation of its scientific name of *Crex crex* which has been likened to running your fingernail along the teeth of a comb, or the eerie wailing of the goggle-eyed stone-curlew. Add the hooting and screeching of owls, and there's still plenty to listen to once the sun has gone down.

But there are out and out songsters who sing in the hours of darkness, birds that are the subject of one of the most persistent cases of mistaken identity in British birding, and one of them is in grave danger of disappearing from our islands altogether.

I've never been described as a party animal, and New Year's Eve is rarely a big deal for me, not least because, for many years, I've spent it preparing to get up early on New Year's Day on a quest to see the year's first birds. But a few years ago, I decided to celebrate with friends at a restaurant in Leicester, and after seeing in the New Year on the little dance floor (strictly eighties disco hits), I went outside for a breath of fresh air.

As I stood amongst the smokers and taxi-seeking couples, at 2 a.m. on a freezing morning, I could hear the unmistakable sound of a robin singing. A quick scan around revealed the singer, perched in the top of a rowan tree in a nearby car park, carolling the revellers on their way home.

Look up this phenomenon online and you'll find plenty of suggestions that robins sing at night because street lights create an artificial daylight that triggers their song response, and their night-time singing is the result of increasing development and urbanisation. While this can't be strictly true, as accounts of robins singing at night date back well into the nineteenth century, including in R.D. Blackmore's 1869 novel *Lorna Doone*, there's little doubt that the absence of genuine darkness in our towns and cities has had some effect and led to an increase in incidences, while another urban factor – noise – also seems to play a part. Robins, research suggests, have cottoned on to the fact that they're far more likely to be heard in the hours of darkness, when towns and cities are quieter.

Widespread and well-documented as this habit is, it's not common knowledge, which means the casual, non-birding listener tends to identify these nocturnal singers as the one species that everyone knows sings at night; a species that is, indeed, defined by it – the nightingale.

The name 'nightingale' is Anglo-Saxon in origin and means 'night songstress', as it was assumed the female did the singing, although it's the male – specifically, the unpaired male – that does so. The nightingale's endlessly inventive mixture of whistles, trills and gurgles is both astonishingly pure and extremely loud; in Spain, where the birds are widespread and numerous, their name is 'ruiseñor' – literally, 'the noisy man'. The volume is required because these lovesick bachelors are, initially at least, trying to attract passing females who are flying over their territory on migration, and later to gain the attention of those unpaired females scattered around the countryside.

Let's return to our city-based, night-time serenaders. The nightingale is not given to frequenting urban environments. It might, conceivably, find something to its liking in one of the larger, wilder city parks, such as London's Hampstead Heath – but as for the small, manicured rectangles of greenery that punctuate our cities and towns, the roundabouts and verges and central reservations of our ring roads, and the gardens of our homes? Forget about it.

This fact was acknowledged by Eric Maschwitz and Manning Sherwin, writers of the song 'A Nightingale Sang in Berkeley Square', a great favourite during the Second World War. The song's whole point, of course, is that the singer is willing to believe all manner of unlikely things could have happened on the magical evening he met his beloved: a nightingale singing in London's West End is every bit as implausible, the song suggests, as angels dining at The Ritz.

The war also, incidentally, provided a remarkable example of the power of birdsong to transcend even the most trying of circumstances. Since 1924, the BBC had been broadcasting, and selling recordings of, the renowned cellist Beatrice Harrison as she played her cello in her garden in Oxted, Surrey to the accompaniment of the nightingales singing there.

In 1942, the broadcast was going ahead as usual, when the microphones started to pick up the drone of approaching aircraft: RAF bombers on the way to attack Mannheim in Germany. As the menacing noise grew louder, so too did the singing of the birds, determined to be heard no matter what. Concerned that any Germans listening in might get warning of the coming raid, a sound engineer abruptly pulled the plug, and radios fell silent across Britain.

To hear the recording now is extraordinary; the nightingales are both a reminder that life – the life of the natural world – carried on as usual despite the tragedies engulfing Europe, as well as being a symbol, perhaps, of the idealised Britain that was being fought for. It's difficult to listen to it without choking back a tear. But birdsong of all sorts can have that effect. Somehow, rather like poetry, it slips past the brain's rational gatekeeper, and attaches itself directly to the emotional core instead.

On a cool evening later in April, I'm at the Knepp Castle Estate, in the West Sussex Weald, where a rather extraordinary rewilding programme is offering new hope that the nightingale won't fall silent in the UK altogether.

The purity and volume of the nightingale's song are partly due to the fact that the sound needs to carry as far as possible in the nightingale's very specialised habitat – coppiced woodland of a particular age, and scrubby thicket of a particular structure, in which they sing from the most impenetrable parts. The lack of such a habitat is one of the reasons why the nightingale has struggled to thrive in Britain in recent years, with only an estimated 6,500 males present each spring and summer, down from perhaps half as many again in the mid-1990s; moreover, the bird is also near the northern edge of its range in West Sussex, with most nightingales confined to the south-east of Britain and East Anglia.

Global warming could play a part in reversing recent declines and extend that range northwards; but in the meantime there are success stories. Paxton Pits, a nature reserve next to a working gravel quarry in Cambridgeshire, is a renowned hotspot, and other old gravel pits are similarly attractive to the birds, because once these areas have been returned to nature they develop at a certain point into exactly the habitat that the nightingales are looking for.

Significantly, both of the nightingale's preferred habitats are very transient. As coppiced trees age they shade out the plants beneath them, leaving the ground-layer too open for nightingales; and a similar thing happens with scrubland. Without the right kind of management to maintain them these habitats disappear – and so do the nightingales.

At Knepp there's an ambitious attempt to use large herbivores to drive landscape changes, with cows, deer, horses and pigs helping to create a mosaic of habitats, including open grassland, regenerating scrub, bare ground and forested groves. Nevertheless, even here there's a recognition that the nightingales will come and go – areas that are good for them one year will eventually be good for other species, while the nightingales will move on in search of their very specific needs. There's a requirement, then, across the country, for new sites to be constantly provided.

Despite their name nightingales do also sing during the day, and on our initial tour of the estate, a good hour-and-a-half before sunset, we catch a couple of snatches of song – remarkably far-carrying on the still air. I begin to understand why this bird has haunted the imaginations of tortured artists and poets for centuries: there's a truly musical beauty to the song, but there's also the resonance added by the apparent hopelessness of their quest (just how likely is a female to be passing?), and the knowledge that any particular nightingale we hear might be gone next year, to another site that meets its very precise requirements.

There's also the sense of time and place that the bird's singing evokes. To hear a nightingale song is to be instantly transported to an evening-time English woodland between mid-April and early June, with all its smells and sounds and sights. Damp earth, and wild garlic, and the new leaves rustling and, here and there, holding on to little pockets of the heat of the day. Bluebells, of course, impossibly, violently violet, pooling around your feet as though the sky has seeped down through the canopy.

It's that way with all birdsong, and perhaps it's one of the reasons why it, and so much of birdwatching generally, can be best appreciated alone. It awakens the poet and artist in all of us, and permits, no – compels, us to take a look inside ourselves.

To hear the nightingale singing in the depths of the night is what really sends a chill down the spine. It's this experience, surely, that has made it such an iconic bird in Western literature and music.

Homer was the first to mention it, in *The Odyssey*, in connection with the myth of Philomela and Procne (Philomel was later used as an alternative name for the bird); and both the Ancient Greek playwright Sophocles and the Roman poet Ovid also wrote their own takes on the myth, in which one of the pair (versions vary) is turned into a nightingale – for that reason, the song was interpreted as a lament, although it's far from the most melancholy of bird songs.

Later poets, from Chaucer – in a poem called 'The Cuckoo and the Nightingale', which acts as a prelude to his longer work *The Parliament of Fowls* – right down to T.S. Eliot in *The Waste Land,* used the same story, while others, including Shakespeare, have tended to use the bird as a symbol of themselves and their own art, with the Bard writing in Sonnet 102:

> Our love was new, and then but in the spring,
> When I was wont to greet it with my lays;
> As Philomel in summer's front doth sing,
> And stops his pipe in growth of riper days ...

By the early nineteenth century, when the Romantic movement was in full swing, the nightingale was again being co-opted by men with time, pens and paper on their hands, representing nothing less than the voice of nature itself. Shelley, in his 'A Defence of Poetry', wrote:

> A poet is a nightingale who sits in darkness and sings to cheer its own solitude with sweet sounds; his auditors are as men entranced by the melody of an unseen musician, who feel that they are moved and softened, yet know not whence or why.

Keats's 'Ode to a Nightingale' similarly portrays the bird as the poet himself would have liked to have been perceived – as the creator of a deathless music that lives on long after him. However, at least one of Keats's contemporaries might have wondered if the bird that inspired the writing of the poem (in Hampstead) was really a nightingale at all. Even if it was, he'd certainly have objected to the way Keats used it largely symbolically, emphasising the effect of its song on him.

That man, John Clare, was the son of a farm labourer from Helpston, Northamptonshire. Almost entirely self-taught, he pursued a number of menial occupations, but also wrote poetry from an early age. After being published by the same company that published Keats, he was for a time a literary sensation. Clare's main subject was the natural world, and the threats he saw being posed to it, especially by the enclosure of common land. Feeling alienated both from literary society and the agricultural workers he'd grown up with, he spent long hours wandering the countryside around his home, and writing about the wildlife he found there, which he described with the skill of one who knew it well. During the last fifty years, his reputation has gradually grown again, with his factual, first-hand and utterly unsentimental approach apparent in the work of poets such as Ted Hughes, as well as in the writings of many nature writers.

It's still possible to hear nightingales singing in good numbers at Castor Hanglands, a nature reserve within sight of the spire of Helpston Church, so perhaps not surprisingly they cropped up again and again in Clare's writing. In 'The Nightingale's Nest' for example, he writes:

> Of summer's fame she shared, for so to me
> Did happy fancies shapen her employ:
> But if I touched a bush, or scarcely stirred,
> All in a moment stopt. I watched in vain:
> The timid bird had left the hazel bush,
> And at a distance hid to sing again.

I find myself thinking of these lines at Knepp. After a lull at sunset and the first ninety minutes or so of darkness the nightingales have started up again, always seemingly just beyond the next hedge, or just over the next rise, always leading us further into the night.

Nevertheless, it's exhilarating to stand there in the dark, ears straining for the next sound. Occasionally there's the distant hooting of tawny owls, and once the screeching of a barn owl, but otherwise the silence is all the deeper for the confidence and élan with which it's shattered every now and then by the nightingales, just as every note of their songs (and the number they pack into each one is astonishing) is thrown into sharper relief by the stillness that surrounds them. The nightingale, like all the best musicians, knows that what you leave out is just as important as what you put in.

I wait until the cold and a pressing appointment first thing in the morning have grown too much to ignore, then head home in the knowledge that the nightingales will be singing right through until dawn. Indeed, dawn and dusk chorus are alike to them – and so is everything in between. They're not, if I'm honest, my favourite British songster – the humble blackbird would win that accolade – but I defy anyone to hear just one nightingale and not feel that they've been touched, for a moment, by the poetry of nature.

3 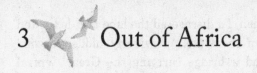 Out of Africa

It's a bitterly cold Sunday at the end of March, and I'm about to indulge in one of my rare bouts of twitching. A lesser scaup, a North American duck, has somehow been blown right across the Atlantic and come to rest in the middle of Leicestershire. I often feel rather uneasy about going to see such 'vagrants', because in the case of many species, especially songbirds, they're never going to be able to make the trip back to their natural homes, but it's different for ducks, which can always take a break any time they feel like it as they cross the ocean. And, anyway, lesser scaups are part of a family very much given to hybridisation – 'love the one you're with' might be their motto – so even if this bird stays here, it isn't necessarily going to be condemned to a lonely, companionless existence before being singled out for the attentions of a peregrine or some other predator with an eye for a stranger. Conscience well and truly squared, I make the short drive from home to Swithland Reservoir, a dozen miles away on the edge of the Soar Valley.

It's a site I visit a lot anyway. Always have, in fact. When I was a child, we'd occasionally stop here on the way back from shopping trips to Leicester, to stand and watch and feed the ducks that gather where the road goes across a little causeway. I don't recall any particular sightings from those days, but in its own small way it must have helped nurture the seeds of my love of birds. When, in the late nineties and early noughties, I returned to birdwatching in earnest, the reservoir became a regular haunt. By then, I'd discovered the lane that led round the larger section of the water, previously hidden beyond a wooded island and a bridge carrying the Great Central Railway's steam trains. You could follow the lane all the way onto the dam, then get good views across the whole expanse of water.

In winter, the water would be thronged with great crested grebes, coots, and ducks such as goldeneye, the pied, posturing males warming up for the breeding season by practising their displays, which involve throwing their heads back as if in silent laughter. In summer, common terns nested on an artificial raft and fished in the filter pools behind the dam, passing just a few feet overhead on their journeys to and fro, while clouds of swallows, martins and swifts hoovered up the mass of insect life swarming over the water. At all times, peregrines and ravens were a possibility. And, even if nothing avian appeared, it was somewhere to go where you could reasonably expect to see no one other than the odd birder, walker, cyclist, or fisherman. In the crowded East Midlands, little oases of calm like that can be hard to come by.

Today is different. That much is obvious from well down the lane, and, as I turn the last corner onto the dam, I can see that, if I am quick, I might just grab the last parking space. The space is tucked immediately behind the old Victorian pumping-house that juts out into the water, and which puts paid to any plans for doing my birding from within a warm car – but beggars can't be choosers.

Inadequately wrapped up against the cold – optimism has triumphed over experience – I set up my scope at a good viewing spot, and start scanning. Very quickly, about two hundred yards away on the water, I come across the lesser scaup, and for a minute or two admire its neat black and white plumage and the way its glossy head appears alternately dark green and dark purple as it turns in the sunlight. The wonders of Austrian optical technology even help pick out the dark vermiculations – thin, wavy stripes – on the white back and wings.

But, and I don't want you to think that I'm overly cynical here, when all's said and done this bird is not so very different from the tufted ducks I can see scattered across the rest of the reservoir, diving and preening. It's even gravitating towards them, no doubt with a view to striking up a transatlantic romance.

So I lift my head from the scope a moment and think about scanning the nearby wood for jays or even lesser spotted woodpeckers, when my eye is caught by the flick of a tail and a flash of white on the top corner of the pumping-house, as something flies in from behind me then disappears behind the parapet. A pied wagtail, perhaps – this corner of the reservoir is a favourite spot for these bold, inquisitive birds, which in summer will occasionally even approach and pick the dead insects off your car bonnet and windscreen.

Then it comes fully into view, shuffling to a halt along the little stone ledge, and I can see it's no wagtail. Grey back, black wings, buffy breast and white underparts, a black eye stripe and, as it turns, a startlingly white rump that identifies it as a wheatear.

The white parts, in fact, are all the more noticeable because, on the whole, this looks like a bird that's been through the wars. It looks wet, just the right side of bedraggled even, and it's got none of the rounded shape you'd usually expect of the species, or of any of the chat family. This bird is positively skinny. I can see its chest expanding and contracting fast, like a panting dog, and it darts its head rapidly this way and that, taking in its new surroundings.

In an instant, the lesser scaup's wanderings from New World to Old recede into the background, and another even more remarkable circumnavigation takes its place in my mind's eye, as it occurs to me that this bird – no bigger than a robin – has literally just touched down after the long flight from somewhere south of the Sahara. No wonder it's not looking its best.

That's not the end of it, either. This isn't its final destination. If it's going to find a mate and raise a family, it's going to have to carry on, at the very least making the short hop to the Peak District, but maybe beyond that, over mountain and sea to Scotland or Iceland or even, incredibly, Canada.

And we think flying a couple of hours to Spain for a summer break is a long haul …

Given what a key role migration plays in the lives of British birds (or perhaps that should be 'British' birds), it's surprising how sketchily this activity is understood, even by those of us happy to be described as birdwatchers.

On the other hand, we're all familiar enough with the concept that we can use an expression such as 'one swallow doesn't make a summer' without any fear of being misunderstood; the implication being that swallows are visitors to these shores whose arrival heralds summer, and whose departure is inevitably associated with the smoky, shortening days of late September.

True enough. Or just about. The first swallows usually make their appearance along the south coast in late March, before the main arrival in the first half of April, so they're more properly a herald of spring. The swift, which often arrives as late as mid-May, and can be gone again by late July, is a far more convincing symbol of the British summer and its infuriating briefness.

But there's far more to migration than that. Britain's just as notable for the birds that visit it in winter, when the country's damp yet mild climate makes it a positively balmy getaway for those species nesting north of the Arctic Circle. The Gulf Stream ensures we're much warmer – and therefore ice- and snow-free – than most places on a similarly northerly latitude and, for the most part, birds don't travel any further south than they need to.

Then there are what's known as passage migrants, those birds that stop off in these islands only briefly, on their way to and from breeding and wintering sites. Our location, just off the north-west corner of the main European landmass, is at something of a crossroads of winds and ocean currents, meaning that in avian terms Britain can resemble a huge hub airport, especially during the peak migration periods in April and October, with constant arrivals and departures as species land to refuel on their way elsewhere.

There are partial migrants, those species in which only some individuals move, or in which all the individuals move but only when faced with extreme weather or food shortages. These can include seemingly familiar species such as the blackbird, with studies showing that many blackbirds in eastern Britain move down to the south-west of the country during cold weather, to be replaced by incomers from Europe and Scandinavia. Weather is relative, after all. What a Norfolk blackbird thinks of as impossibly cold, a Norwegian blackbird might consider merely a bit parky. The same principle, it seems, is behind the increasing frequency with which blackcaps are seen in our gardens in winter. Our own blackcaps, in fact, are still heading south to the Med for some winter sun, but somewhat counter-intuitively they're being replaced by visually indistinguishable

German birds, happy to swap the snowbound forests of Bavaria and Thuringia for the suburban estates of East Anglia and our mild, maritime climate.

And finally there are the other summer visitors, the birds that don't ever achieve the same sort of headlines as swallows, nightingales, swifts or cuckoos, but which nonetheless year after year make long flights from south of the Mediterranean or in many cases south of the Sahara. Warblers such as the garden warbler or whitethroat. Songbirds such as the redstart or pied flycatcher. Seabirds such as the Arctic tern. Even birds of prey, such as the hobby.

Just to confuse things further, species often fit into more than one of these categories. Black-tailed godwits, for example, breed in small numbers, but these islands are also host to a substantial wintering population from Iceland and the far north, as well as passage birds moving between those northern sites and wintering areas in Portugal and Spain. Bird-ringing – in which birds are trapped and have a numbered metal ring fitted round their legs before being released – has shown that those spending time here are willing to move from one side of the country to the other on a daily basis, as weather and food availability demand.

Migration, then, is more than merely an activity carried out by birds a couple of times a year. It defines, for many of them, what they are: creatures of seemingly perpetual motion, bound forever to an invisible network of flyways criss-crossing the globe, in thrall to the seasons and the vagaries of the weather. It's both their curse and their blessing, and it's without doubt what makes them so fascinating to us, hopelessly bound as we are by the ties of family, work, place and culture.

Wheatears, like the one I saw at Swithland Reservoir, are among the pioneers of the yearly spring migration, outriders of a vast bird movement that aims to take advantage of the short but exceptionally fecund summer in the northern hemisphere. The first bird can appear as early as the opening week of March, and certainly by mid-month scattered reports start coming in from everywhere, along with sightings of sand martins and little ringed plovers, two more species that have taken to heart the old adage about early birds catching the worm.

With wheatears, their northward movement continues well into May, because in addition to the birds that breed on our own upland pastures and rocky slopes, we host those who are bound for Scandinavia, Greenland and eastern Canada. Our breeders have varying needs, too – a bird breeding in the Peak District will probably arrive well ahead of one that nests in the Cairngorm glens. That extended migration period, however, means that wheatears tend to be seen in dribs and drabs.

Not so some of our other summer visitors. It's now the third week in April, and we're just about reaching the peak of the migration period. If I were at home, I'd probably be racing around my inland patch trying to see small numbers of redstarts, yellow wagtails and ring ouzels as they pass through, ticking off a few of the commoner warblers as I do so.

I'm not, though. You'd think a lifelong fixation with birds and birdwatching – and all the ribbing regarding nerdy, anorak-wearing stereotypes that this inspires – would be enough for any man, but somewhere along the line I've found myself joining the ranks of another group of people who, in modern Britain, inspire amusement and consternation in equal measure at the mere mention of their name. It started in my teens, with odd bits of doggerel in imitation of my favourite bands, and before I knew it I was on to the hard stuff, scribbling sonnets in my lunch hour. I'm a poet, not to mention a sucker for punishment.

If you can ride the jibes, there are plenty of consolations to pursuing the path of poetry. Not the financial kind, obviously, but then that spares poets like me all that agonised soul-searching over whether something as vulgar as money hopelessly compromises their art. No, I'm thinking more of the pleasure of creating something from scratch, the satisfaction of occasionally meeting someone who likes your work, the feeling of being part of a like-minded community of writers, and the buzz of occasionally getting up on stage and reading your verse to total strangers.

That part, for me, has another built-in bonus. My intermittent jaunts around the country on the poetry 'circuit' can usually be combined with some excellent birding, especially as several of the best poetry festival venues are at locations such as Aldeburgh or St Andrews, ornithological hotspots both.

On this occasion, I've just read at Lewes, near Brighton, and with the weather set fair, I decide not to head straight back via the nightmare of the M25 and M1, but instead to work my way west along the south coast, then turn up past Winchester and Newbury and Oxford. My expectations aren't particularly high – being out and about on a warm, sunny day will be reward enough, and if a few migrants cross my path at the same time, so much the better.

Having pottered around Newhaven, I make my way to Bosham on Chichester Harbour, mainly with the intention of seeing the small but distinctive church that appears in the Bayeux Tapestry. While there I watch as a solitary little tern, an early arrival well ahead of his fellows, hovers and plunge-dives into the sparkling water, only after ten attempts finally coming up with a tiny strand of silver in its beak.

This sight, for a sea-starved Midlander like me, would normally feel like hitting pay dirt, but I'm hungry for more. Although the sky has clouded over and there's a stiff southerly breeze blowing, I've got time to drive out towards Selsey Bill, stopping at Pagham Harbour on the way. This area – the harbour itself, as well as Sidlesham Ferry and Church Norton – have always been popular with birdwatchers, so it's time to find out what all the fuss is about. Again, in my mind, I'm setting the bar low. A scattering of waders – any waders – would leave a smile on my face all the way home, and as I climb out of the car I wonder if I dare hope for something in the way of songbirds. A redstart, perhaps?

I've walked perhaps twenty yards from the lane towards the main lagoon when a movement in the scrubby hedge catches my eye. I raise my binoculars, focus, and the view is filled with the gorgeously contrasting tones of a male redstart, the rusty-red breast and the ash-grey back and head, both set off by the black throat and white forehead. And of course there's the red tail, the *steort* that, in Anglo-Saxon times, gave the bird its name. Like the wheatear (to which it's closely related), this is a species that winters south of the Sahara, before returning to our deciduous woodlands to breed; and, taking in its beautiful, bright colours, it doesn't take too much of a stretch to imagine yourself watching a bird such as this on the edge of an African savannah. That's not to say that British birds can't be colourful, gaudy, even; but redstarts are birds that almost demand to be spot-lit by dazzling midday sun falling through the leaves of acacia trees, rather than fluffing themselves up against the sea-fret that's just blown them across the Channel.

So, a very good start. In fact, so serendipitous does the encounter seem – think of a bird, see it seconds later – that I briefly wonder whether I could run through the field guide in my mind and subsequently tick off a whole series of bogey birds.

Turns out I'm rather missing the point. However special a redstart is, or the yellow wagtail that scurries from cowpat to cowpat just ahead of me, as isolated examples of the migratory impulse they don't bring home the message of quite how extraordinary, and how enormous, that twice-yearly transference of biomass from one hemisphere to another is.

An appreciation of this comes with the sight that meets my gaze as I skirt the lagoon itself, where the path passes between the water and a little caravan park. The seaward side of the lagoon is dotted by small trees every few yards, and as I approach the first one I assume that the whispering I can hear is just the wind in the new leaves. Only as I turn to look properly do I realise that the whole tree is shivering with what must be at least fifty excited, restless willow warblers. The faint, sibilant noise is a combination of thin contact calls and the flutter of tiny, tired wings wearily taking flight to the next tree along.

It's obvious that these birds, each no bigger than a blue tit, have just made landfall after their flight from France: like many small birds, they'll have made their longer journey, from tropical Africa, in a number of stages, stopping off whenever necessary to feed and rest, and always waiting for the wind to turn in the right direction for them to hitch a lift on Mother Nature's coat-tails. As I scan along the trees, away into the distance, I can see that each one is similarly alive with these tiny songsters, neat and quietly beautiful in their green-brown, pale yellow and white finery.

What's most astonishing, perhaps, is that despite arrivals such as this, which make the willow warbler one of Britain and northern Europe's commonest birds in the spring and summer, it's a species that almost entirely fails to register on the radar of non-birdwatchers. These birds, and the thousands and thousands more that will arrive along the south coast over a period of a few days (there are more than 2 million breeding territories in the UK), will move inland, spreading out like a fanned wing, with birds dropping off as and when they reach their old breeding areas. There they'll spend the short months of summer feverishly working to raise a family, occasionally even two, before the whole daunting return journey begins again as early as the end of July.

And they'll do it all without attracting the attention of the Great British Public. Even birdwatchers won't give them too many second glances.

In the case of birds making this round trip for the first time, they'll have the added anxiety of knowing they need to find new territories, new mates. In recent years in Britain, habitat has been squeezed and numbers have fallen, but the north of the country – especially Scotland, with its extensive birch woodlands – remains a stronghold; and perhaps the majority of the birds I'm seeing will end up there, silvering the glens and mountainsides with their ripplingly melodic song, which begins high-pitched and faint, builds to a crescendo, then descends to a slower, sadder ending. It's both familiar – somewhat recalling the song of the ubiquitous chaffinch – and yet wistful, ungraspable, with a plaintive quality that a chaffinch, perhaps, could only hope to achieve if it too had travelled half the world and seen all its sorrows on the way.

As I stand, a willow warbler sings. Shyly and hesitantly at first, testing itself against memory and weariness and the growing cold of the Sussex afternoon. And then another, and another, and another takes up the song, and there's no way back. The season cycle has moved into a higher gear.

In spring, scenes like this occur along the whole of the south coast. When the wind is right, which is to say from the south and south-west, huge 'falls' of migrants can occur as backed-up bird traffic floods in from the continent. Headlands such as Beachy Head and Selsey Bill in Sussex, and Berry Head in Devon, can be the best places to look, as the birds naturally make for whatever piece of land is most visible to them from far out to sea; but in truth they can arrive absolutely anywhere. Vegetation is important – it provides cover for the new arrivals, and will be a source of the insect food that they need – but at times the old adage 'any port in a storm' applies.

At some of those aforementioned headlands, such as Dungeness and Portland Bill, birdwatchers and ornithologists have long taken advantage of birds' liking of these sites as ports of entry, in order to carry out a huge, ongoing citizen science project. Incoming birds can be trapped with fine mist nets without being harmed, before being ringed. Some of these birds – actually a fairly small percentage – will subsequently be trapped again, and the information on their location will be fed back to the original ringing site. Similarly, the rings from birds found dead are often returned to the organisations that ringed them. It's this, above all, that over the last hundred years or so has enabled us to start to understand the sheer scale and variety of bird migration.

Or so we thought. In recent years advances in technology have enabled birders and scientists to fit electronic geo-locators to birds. These, originally fitted to large birds such as ospreys, transmit the bird's exact location (and sometimes certain information about that location) at least a couple of times a day, enabling those studying the bird to get an exact picture, and map, of its movements.

As always in the modern world, the technology has rapidly got smaller, less heavy and intrusive, allowing it to be used

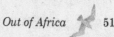

on lighter birds without affecting their ability to fly. Perhaps the most remarkable results of all, so far, have come from the British Trust for Ornithology's Cuckoo Project, which set out to discover if any of the reasons for this iconic species' worrying decline were to be found along its migration route, rather than simply on its British breeding grounds.

The first surprise was just what that migration route was. In the first batch of birds to be tracked, all selected from nests in East Anglia, some took a central European route, passing down through Italy and then hopping across the Mediterranean via Malta (a hazardous undertaking, given the scale of illegal hunting on that island). Others, though, passed down through France and Spain, crossing the Med at or close to the Straits of Gibraltar. All, from that first batch of six, made it across the forbidding barrier of the Sahara Desert.

This would be fascinating and revealing in any species, but in the case of the cuckoo it's all the more remarkable because of the fact that the birds – all youngsters making the journey for the first time – had to do so entirely on their own initiative. Cuckoos, of course, never see their real mothers or fathers, having been brought up by unfortunate foster parents such as dunnocks, or meadow pipits, most of which don't make a sub-Saharan migration; so there's no chance of these juveniles making the journey as part of a family group – something that happens, for example, with geese. And, as the geo-locators showed, our own cuckoos don't migrate in flocks, as some of their more exotic relatives do, such as the huge channel-billed cuckoo of Australia and New Guinea.

The prospect of similar, even tinier tracking devices being fitted to very small birds should provide vital information that could shape conservation work for years to come.

And the scope of such projects is absolutely huge. Take the house martin. Even if the average non-birdwatcher might mix it up with the swallow, the swift, and the sand martin, it's familiar to most of us, not least because of its habit of living under the eaves of houses. In recent years, however, it's undergone a worrying decline in the UK, and researchers are keen to discover how much our human habits have to do with that. Dryer springs certainly haven't helped, as the house martins need plenty of wet mud for building their nests, but there's a suspicion that the major cause is that, in these house-proud times, people aren't keen on having mud plastered all over their fascia boards. If that is the case, there's a simple potential solution, as similar and closely related species in North America have long used artificial nests happily.

Amazingly, given that house martins must have lived in close proximity to man since not long after we moved out of caves, we still have no clear idea where they spend the winter. While swallows can end up as far south as Cape Town, and many of our warblers travel to the Sahel, the semi-arid zone of grassland and scrub that divides the Sahara from the savannahs further south, the destination of house martins remains a mystery. The tentative suggestion is that they end up high over the forests of central Africa, enjoying the endless supply of insect food there, but no one really knows for sure. Soon, with the help of new technology, we could put that right, and perhaps discover whether some hitherto unknown factor on the wintering grounds is also affecting populations.

Whether it's through ringing, geo-tagging, or any other method (in Israel, for example, military radars are used to plot the approach of migrating flocks of cranes and pelicans, to enable food to be provided for them), there's a point at which the simple act of watching birds becomes something more active, more loaded with intent and the possibility of putting right some of the unintended but immense harm we've done to bird populations in the past couple of industrial centuries. And

such conservation-minded birding is often, for me, the most rewarding part of the pastime, because it's an opportunity to appreciate the vast scale of nature, and your own insignificance within it.

As it started, so it ends. Towards the end of April, I'm fitting a hurried hour's tramp around my favourite local reserve – an old sewage works called Kelham Bridge – into a busy Sunday.

On a small sward of short-cropped grass on the little hill above the reserve, the unmistakable white flash of the wheatear is the first thing I see as I walk up the path. Presumably having enjoyed at least a couple of weeks in which to replenish its reserves, this one's plumper, neater and altogether more pristine than the waif that dropped into Swithland back in March, and it looks in no hurry to move on.

Wheatears are easy birds to admire, even without taking into consideration their astounding feats of globetrotting. Quite apart from physical beauty, they create the impression of energy and purpose, and of quiet confidence – they're watchful without ever being too quick to flush at the sight of man.

And then there's the name. For all that it conjures up the image of golden fields of corn waving in a gentle summer breeze – there's a ripening wheat field in the distance beyond this bird – the name actually has a much earthier, but no less poetic, derivation.

Wheatears must have been familiar to the Anglo-Saxons from their ancestral homelands of northern Germany and Jutland, and when they arrived in Britain they brought their name for the species (and for many others) with them. They were a warrior race as well as subsistence farmers, and you can't imagine they had too much time for considering the finer points of bird identification, so they developed the admirable habit of fixing on one striking characteristic and naming with that in mind. In this case, *hvit oers*. White arse.

Over many centuries, this became eroded to something like the current name, before the delicate sensibilities of Victorian naturalists brought a final smoothing away of any lingering bawdiness. A wheat field, at any time of year, is actually a pretty unlikely place to find them. A nearby sheep pasture, on the other hand, as here, is perfect.

I turn to go, wondering where this particular bird's final destination might be, and as I do, the most instantly recognisable birdsong in the western world rings out somewhere along the valley. The resonant, querulous song of the cuckoo, a call with only one meaning.

Spring.

4 Fleeing the Waters

From where I'm standing, it's the shallow, pencilled V of a child's drawing, but far from being the anonymous, generic bird of such scribbles, it's instantly recognisable to every one of us gathered along the edge of the rain-slicked road that fronts a seemingly unremarkable expanse of windswept saltmarsh. It hugs the contours of the ground exactly, rising or falling mere millimetres in response to every tussock of rough grass, every murky channel and rivulet, the flat disc of its face always turned towards the waterlogged earth.

When it nears us on the pavement, it turns and banks slightly, and the flash of a bright white rump tells us what we already knew. It's a hen harrier, a female or juvenile. They lack the striking pale grey plumage of the male, being a streaky dark brown, but they lose nothing by comparison where grace and elegance are concerned. And they're every bit as difficult to find, with the result that birdwatchers relish every encounter with them.

Back in the eighteenth century, the females and juveniles of this species, and the females and juveniles of the closely related Montagu's harrier (a more southern European bird, which breeds in Britain in tiny numbers), were considered part of the same species: the 'ringtail harrier', with the males similarly grouped together as a second species, the 'ash-coloured harrier'. They were finally separated by the naturalist George Montagu, who noticed not only the small but significant differences in plumage and structure, but also that the Montagu's harrier was a bird of open grasslands (and occasionally standing crops), while the hen harrier was a creature of the uplands.

And that's where naturalists started noticing a problem. Much of Britain's moorland is used for rearing and shooting grouse, and increasingly, moving towards modern times, these have been large-scale, driven shoots, in which relatively large numbers of people pay a lot of money to pick off a lot of birds. Hen harriers, which do take a certain amount of young grouse, but which also prey heavily on rodents and small birds, are seen as the enemy by some, perhaps most, estates, and so have faced persecution from gamekeepers. The opposing argument is that the habitat management and conservation work that the grouse require are beneficial to the harriers too – and on the face of it there's something in that – but the absurdly low number of hen harriers found around areas of intensive grouse shooting would seem to give the lie to that particular theory.

Every time I see a hen harrier, and it's not often these days, all this runs through my mind. And so it does today, as the bird banks away from me, its attention fixed so firmly on the watery world beneath it that it pays me no more heed than it does one of the fence posts.

As it glides away, other shapes, dark blurs over the outer reaches of the marsh, start to come into focus. Heart-faced barn owls, three of them, white against the distant sea as they ghost towards us, buoyant on the stiff breeze. Short-eared owls, the orange patches on the underside of their long wings flashing every time they flap, their yellow eyes blazing fire at us when our scopes catch their gazes. A merlin, smallest of British birds of prey, motionless for a moment on a fence post, then bouncing low above the ground in imitation of a thrush. A peregrine, too, happy to abandon the glamour of its high-velocity dive for once, instead hunting by ambush like a sparrowhawk, chasing waders flushed by the rising waters. More hen harriers, ringtails all, sadly. A few grey herons stand sentinel, presumably reflecting that the waters still have a couple of feet to rise before they need to worry. Above us, buzzards soar and kestrels hover, as only they can, and carrion crows, magpies and an assortment of gulls, the supreme opportunists of the avian world, swirl overhead or perch prominently.

They're not the only predators out there. We spot a stoat weaving through the grass towards us, the black tip of its tail quivering every time it pauses. Excitement, perhaps, or more likely cold, because its slicked-down coat suggests it's had a close call where the onrushing waters are concerned.

And first one, then two foxes emerge from behind a large tussock, and start picking their way through the pools and rivulets that the advancing tide is creating. For a moment, it looks as though one of them has marooned itself and will be forced to swim for it. It pauses atop a hummock, swiftly glancing all around. Not for nothing do foxes have a reputation for wiliness and resourcefulness, however. Having quickly sized up the situation, it makes an extravagant leap, briefly splashing down on a just-covered tussock, and another jump to reach a thin strand of dry land. Relieved at its escape, it makes haste in our direction, without looking back at the easy meals it might be leaving behind, or maybe it has already eaten well enough.

Because that's what this is all about. For every predator, in winter and spring especially, each day is a constant struggle to solve a single calorific equation, and what happens at this otherwise unremarkable stretch of coastline a few times each year presents them with an opportunity to short-circuit the whole system and tap into a sudden, natural glut. For us standing here, it's a chance to see some often-shy species at close quarters, while considering the way we view the relationship between hunter and hunted.

A lot of Britain's best birdwatching spots are saltmarshes, or contain saltmarsh, or adjoin saltmarshes. Among them, Parkgate, on the Wirral coast of the Dee estuary, doesn't at first appear to be anything out of the ordinary. In fact, it appears a good deal less interesting than most.

Not that there's anything wrong with the Wirral, of course, notwithstanding the rather unflattering description of its inhabitants given by the anonymous poet who wrote *Sir Gawain and the Green Knight* in the fourteenth century:

> The wilderness of Wirral:
> few lived there
> Who loved with a good heart
> Either God or man

No, these days, it's a thoroughly salubrious place to be, with pleasant towns, villages and suburbs, prestigious golf courses, and a wealth of good bird habitats. The Dee estuary coast has marshes, mudflats and therefore plenty of waders; the blunt tip of land is a great spot to look for passing seabirds; and in autumn the Mersey shore is sometimes the place to see large numbers of Leach's petrels, miniature albatrosses skimming and almost dancing on the water – they're funnelled into the estuary when gales strike just as they're migrating south down Britain's west coasts.

All good, but what makes Parkgate stand out? You can't get right out into the midst of the marsh, as you can at some reserves, where boardwalks, raised paths and hides have long allowed birders a closer view. At Parkgate, you do your viewing from the promenade, or from the Old Baths car park, because to venture onto the marsh at any time of year would risk disturbing – 'putting up', to use a phrase which birdwatchers have, rather curiously, borrowed from the shooting fraternity – every bird out there. These could number, at certain times, hundreds upon thousands of waders and wildfowl. Moreover, leaving the safety of the tarmac would also put you at risk of another thing that makes Parkgate so fascinating. Its tides.

Britain as a whole has some of the highest tidal ranges in the world, one of the reasons we're such a popular destination for those waders and wildfowl. Twice every twenty-four hours the ocean uncovers wide acres of mudflat and saltmarsh newly replenished with all kinds of sea creatures, from fish, crustaceans and the like, to tiny micro-organisms.

Now, any high tide, anywhere, is generally good for birdwatching, because it tends to force birds that would otherwise stay way out on the shore or estuary to come in much closer to dry ground. And any high tide at Parkgate is good, because the Dee estuary and the Wirral are a bird-rich area anyway, and Parkgate has a wide tidal range. But a few times a year, and especially when a high spring tide arrives, it's the stage for a truly extraordinary wildlife spectacle. And that's what's happening today.

First, as with every tide, it moves the birds. A thin smoke of waders lifts from the far edges of the marsh, and drifts upriver and inland. The interest of the peregrines is piqued, but they're willing to wait on this occasion. Next come the starlings, reed buntings, a mixed flock of finches, and a miscellany of other small birds, dashing towards the promenade, keeping low. This time a merlin follows, and three meadow pipits streak away just ahead of it. Two veer right, the other goes left, and for a split-second it must lose sight of the falcon, which follows and comes up from below to snatch it in mid-air. Ducks, geese and other wildfowl, showing the sort of sangfroid that can be afforded by confident and habitual swimmers, move rather more slowly up the saltmarsh, finally stopping to graze when they reach a spot as yet untouched by the sea. Over on the far right edge, a water rail picks its way from one little island to another, its bright red bill revealing its presence, all its usual caution gone.

I'm reminded that, in my experience, water rails might be Britain's most schizophrenic birds. For the vast majority of the time, they're extremely difficult to spot, remaining completely hidden in reed beds and other waterside vegetation. The only reason you know they're there is their disgruntled, pig-like squealing, or the occasional glimpse of a bird creeping from one stand of reeds to another. But when extreme circumstances intervene, that all changes. Once, when visiting Titchwell RSPB in Norfolk during a cold snap that had frozen parts of the lagoons and reed beds, I stood on the path and watched as a water rail probed around in some mud so close to me that I could barely focus my binoculars on it. During another cold spell, at my local reserve, another showed up at similarly close quarters, pecking around under the feeders just outside one of the hides. When a rat, trying to take advantage of the fallen grain and seed, ventured a little too close, the water rail speared it neatly, and started trying to make a meal of it. And then there's the story of one at Parkgate a few years ago, which took refuge in the rucksack of one of the birdwatchers lined up on the promenade ...

But back to the present. Next, the mammals appear. Rabbits, of course, are easily spotted and not at all unexpected, but then a whole hidden stratum of the eco-system arrives – creatures that we know must exist in large numbers to support the raptors and owls and foxes and herons and other predators, but that most of us, including those who spend large parts of their life out in the field, rarely ever have an opportunity to see. Voles and shrews and mice and the occasional rat. In the normal course of things, these rodents live in the upper part of the saltmarsh that the sea never reaches; but the exceptional spring tides can reach the road itself, and at such times there's nothing for them to do but flee further and further inland. If this means running the gauntlet of the assembled predators, not to mention the gathered birdwatchers and photographers, then so be it.

So I watch and watch as the tide gets nearer, while another tide, with sea-sleeked fur, runs a few yards ahead of it. When the latter reaches the wall, finally, the survivors scramble up and past us and, incredibly, brave a further dash across the road towards the nearest cover.

It is astonishing but it's also, I'm surprised to find, genuinely distressing. I say surprised because a lifetime of birdwatching should teach the truth of Alfred, Lord Tennyson's phrase 'Nature, red in tooth and claw', while a liking for the work of another Poet Laureate, Ted Hughes, also tends to destroy any vestiges of sentimentality about nature. Out in the field, you see kestrels snatch voles, buzzards take rabbits. Even when a sparrowhawk ambushes a favourite robin on your garden feeders, or a heron grabs a still-fluffy duckling from under the beak of its distressed mother, you reflect that it's just the way things have to be.

But at Parkgate, the predation is on such a scale, is so relentless, that you start to want to intervene. It's like watching *Saving Private Ryan* while being beaten over the head with a copy of Hughes's *Collected Poems* (and he was extremely prolific). You couldn't do anything, of course, because chances are that most of the terrified creatures would be even more terrified of you if you approached them, but you do start wondering if you couldn't scoop up a few, at least. For the first time in my birdwatching life I find myself emphatically on the side of the hunted.

Birdwatchers tend to like raptors, you see. Perhaps it's exaggerated in Britain, where for centuries numbers were kept artificially low by gamekeepers, and where large birds of prey are still few and far between. But whatever the reason, they're without doubt the stars of the birding scene.

I'm no different. There was the osprey in a school project that played a part in interesting me in birdwatching, and the kestrel that I watched hovering over the lane near our house every time my parents took us kids out walking. But I'd forgotten, until now, that from the age of about nine, right through my teenage years, the walls of my bedroom were covered not with pop stars, or football teams, or film actors and actresses, but with five huge posters bearing drawings of different species of eagle. It wasn't that I didn't like pop music or sport or girls, you understand (and thinking about it, perhaps a single small Leicester City poster and another of batting genius David Gower were there too), and it wasn't that my parents were old fuddy-duddies who insisted I put something educational on the walls. No, it was entirely my choice, and it had everything to do with the aura projected by the birds.

I'd come across birds of prey in a rather mundane source. One Saturday morning, I was with my mother, walking through Leicester on a shopping expedition. It was early, the shops were just opening up, and we were in the quiet streets behind the market that, in those days, held countless banks and insurance companies, but which nowadays are home to umpteen near-identical bars. The identity of different financial institutions meant nothing to me, so when I saw five huge eagle posters in a window, I stopped and took a closer look. Only two of them were species I'd heard of, and I tried to create a mental picture of the other three for future reference before Mum dragged me off to Gallowtree Gate and Marks & Spencer.

As I stood in front of the window, a man in suit and tie came out of the office in question, and asked: 'Do you like them?'

'Yes,' I said, and I imagine my slightly embarrassed mum offered him a few words of explanation about the reasons for my interest.

'Wait here a moment.' He dashed back into the shop, re-emerging moments later with five rolled-up posters. We thanked him profusely, and I clung on to the posters with almost unbearable anticipation until we got home, when I could unroll them and get my dad to Blu-Tack them onto the wall. Golden eagle, white-tailed eagle, harpy eagle, bald eagle and bateleur. The fact that the lower quarter of each of them carried the words Eagle Star Insurance, along with a slogan and a certain amount of sales bumf, mattered not a jot. For the next ten years or so, I would fall asleep each night beneath the piercing and pitiless gaze of some of the world's largest raptors, and that nurtured my undying fascination with them. When, on a recent trip to South Africa, I finally saw the bizarrely tail-less, front-heavy outline of a bateleur over the Kruger National Park, I felt like I knew it as well as any back-garden robin, so constant a companion had it been throughout my teenage years.

There's a word that, I think, sums up the appeal of these birds. Glamour. Not in the modern sense – in which glamour has become the debased currency of film, TV and pop stars, the glittering trappings of lavish lifestyles and sexual allure – but the original meaning, signifying a sort of enchantment which made the subject see things in a different way. Even further back, the word was a variant of 'grammar', and meant any sort of scholarship, particularly occult.

So, when confronted with a bird of prey, most of us, whether birdwatcher or 'civilian', tend to react with a slightly awed reverence. I've seen it all around me at falconry displays. Such reverence is a completely natural reaction to the spectacle of an eagle owl, say, or a golden eagle, where the size of the bird in general, and especially the bill and talons, inspires respect in anyone with enough imagination to picture being at the receiving end of either. Or a peregrine, simply because it's the fastest creature on earth.

But I've also watched as people – from young children through to pensioners – have treated kestrels and barn owls in exactly the same way, with similar levels of awe. Perhaps, with these birds, the reason is because their abilities seem to take on a hint of the supernatural. They're neither huge, nor powerful, yet they're efficient killing machines. Consider the way a kestrel can judge its position, flying into the wind so perfectly that its head remains absolutely motionless, which enables its eyes to pick out the movements of tiny mammals and insects below, often by using its ultraviolet vision to look for traces of their urine. Or the way a barn owl's offset ears are used to triangulate any sounds and pinpoint prey while the bird floats effortlessly over the ground. Add to that the way that all raptors and owls seem to have the same air of grave, detached superiority that cats also affect (with the possible exception of the little owl, which just looks comically ill-tempered), and the fact that they're pretty much the only natural predators we see in Britain, and it's easy to understand why they continue to cast their spell.

But, and maybe this is a bit of a stretch, I wonder whether this also helps explain the persecution that these birds have so often faced. Yes, various raptors do undoubtedly take young game birds. Yes, golden and white-tailed eagles have preyed on lambs, although usually sickly ones that would soon die anyway. Yes, ospreys do take fish from farms and well-stocked fishing lakes. What's difficult to understand is the scale of the depredations attributed to them as justification for large-scale culling. Raptors and owls are talked about as though they're omnipresent and unnaturally hungry, even in the case of smaller birds of prey such as sparrowhawks, which are routinely blamed for the decline of all sorts of small birds. In fact, because they take such a range of prey, from blue tit up to woodpigeon, raptors have next to no impact on populations, except at a very local level. If they did wipe out the small birds in any given area, they'd soon die themselves, for lack of food.

And so, back at Parkgate, where my momentary flirtation with solidarity for prey, rather than predator, comes to an end. It *is* difficult to watch, at times, and you can still feel the appropriate sympathy for those unfortunate creatures destined to die, but it's also an absolutely natural phenomenon.

If too many voles, for example, evade both drowning in the deluge and the claws of their many predators, they might subsequently face a slow, agonising death from hunger – the same death, incidentally, that faces all those predators themselves if they don't take ruthless advantage of this gift of nature.

Only two days after my trip to Parkgate, for example, I find the body of a barn owl on a bridleway near home. It's unmarked, and although barn owls have a habit of hunting along road verges, in this particular instance the bird couldn't have fallen victim to the nemesis of so many of its kind: the motor vehicle. Given its rather emaciated look, it seems to have starved to death. It's not been a cold winter, but perhaps competition for prey locally has been particularly fierce; and a recent spell of wet weather won't have helped, as barn owls have particularly poor waterproofing on their feathers.

In fact, a variety of potential deaths from natural causes is built into the equations that underpin the breeding cycles of all creatures. For the most part, relatively few young of any small bird or animal survive their first year of life, but as long as the number is enough to replace losses in the population, there's no need to worry. The problems only arise when some other factor, not included in nature's calculations, intervenes on one side or another. That other factor, more often than not, is a two-legged, upright creature that tends to forget it's part of a much wider whole.

5   A Bridge Between Two Worlds

Their pristine whiteness is the first thing that strikes me. On an overcast morning at the beginning of May, each high-speed flypast is like an eraser drawn across a scene sketched in the heaviest of pencil tones.

They scissor and slice their way through the slightly damp air, mixing long, elegant glides with light, buoyant flapping, occasionally descending right down to the level of the murky water, before sweeping up and around again. The sooty triangles on each wingtip look like an accumulation of the everyday world's grime and dirt on beings belonging to a more ethereal plane, and the birds' attitude to what's around them only reinforces that impression.

If they're aware that they're right in the middle of a prime example of twenty-first-century urban regeneration, and not on some wind-lashed stack of North Atlantic rock, they give absolutely no indication. Their behaviour is exactly the same as the hundreds of thousands of other members of their species who do frequent the coasts and islands of the British Isles. We city-dwellers might as well not be here. A cliff is a cliff is a six-storey office development with attached parking.

I'm not carrying binoculars, so I have to wait until two birds come in to one of many ledges on a solid, four-square Victorian building that must once have been a shipping merchant's office but is now, inevitably, a restaurant. Then, at close range as they sit on their moss-lined nest, I can see the short, black legs, the neat yellow bill and the 'kind' expression of the eye and forehead, compared with the rather baleful glare of most gulls.

But in truth, and even though gulls generally give me more ID headaches than any other family of birds, I don't need to check. For one thing, every one of the hundred or so birds that are within my frame of vision at any one time has been screaming its name at me throughout: 'K-wake, k-wake, ktiti-wa-a-k. Kittiwake!'

This, the most numerous of Britain's common gull species, is also paradoxically the least typical, the least known (even by birdwatchers), and the least understood in its very particular habits and requirements. Normally, unlike most of its relatives, it wouldn't be seen anywhere near the centre of a modern city, much less raising its young there. This is a truly unique colony.

For another thing, these sleek white apparitions carry with them not only the salt tang of the wide, wild oceans, and the thrill that goes with seeing any genuinely globetrotting bird, but a long trail of memories. They're the ghosts of another spring morning twenty-something years previously, when I first experienced their ability to transport the unwitting observer through space and time, and as I stand and watch I'm gone again ...

If there's one family of birds that divides birdwatchers from the great, rational mass of the population, it's gulls. That they also divide birdwatchers themselves is another story, and one that we'll come to in due course.

Let's start with the name. You can always identify a birdwatcher in any conversation or pub quiz by the way they sigh, tut-tut and give an exasperated look towards the ceiling when a civilian refers to a 'seagull'. There's no such thing, they'll tell you if you give them half a chance (and I'd advise you to start making for the exit the moment they give the first indication of their irritation).

They do have a point, though. By far the most familiar representative of the family in Britain is the black-headed gull, which has the distinction of being inappropriately named by those who really should know better – birders – as well as the general public. For a start, for the majority of the year it has a largely white head, marked with dark smudges that could, given its proclivity for rooting around in garbage, easily be taken for dirt. For another, the smart hood that it develops in late winter and sports throughout the breeding season is actually a dark-chocolate brown.

More importantly for our purposes here, it's a bird whose habitat is far from restricted to coastlines. You'll see them on farmland, either probing away in sheep pastures or following tractors to gobble up insects thrown up by the plough. You'll find them at landfill tips and recycling depots, rooting through mountains of household refuse for tasty morsels. They hang around sewage works, too, where they eat the insects attracted by another kind of human waste. They splash around reservoirs, lakes, rivers and even the smallest ponds and pools, returning to the larger bodies of water at night to roost. And they glide and flap around town centres and retail parks, in patient anticipation of the rich harvest to be reaped from human visitors and their penchant for fast food. At times, it's almost a surprise when you do come across one on a beach or harbour wall.

The same is true, to varying extents, of most of our other gull species. Common gulls turn up on the top of mountains, as well as sharing the black-headed's liking for modern farming methods. Lesser black-backeds and herring gulls can be found loafing on reservoirs as far from the sea as it's possible to get in Britain (and admittedly that's not far for a creature capable of flight), as well as picking their way through rubbish tips, where they're joined by the bullying bruiser that is the great black-backed. Little gulls are as happy in inland wetlands as in a more maritime habitat, although we see them only as they migrate through these islands, when they often cut across country rather than follow the coast.

Britain also plays host to a certain amount of gull visitors from much further afield, and it's usually a mark of a truly dedicated, expert birdwatcher that he or she is willing to spend hours standing in the freezing winter cold at some bleak inland reservoir or landfill to pick out the likes of Mediterranean, yellow-legged, Caspian, Iceland and glaucous gulls from the great mass of more familiar species. Even many who would describe themselves as dyed-in-the-wool birdwatchers balk at the thought of the time, endurance and detailed feather-by-feather analysis needed to identify some of these species. And yes, I count myself among that lily-livered group.

But the one British gull species that genuinely does deserve the name 'seagull' is the kittiwake. They share the same basic look as the rest of the family – white body, largely grey wings, webbed feet, long wings – and so are perhaps unlikely to turn the head of the non-birdwatcher any more than their relatives, but they really do deserve your attention.

Their ease in the air, with a buoyant flying style that sometimes recalls those swallows of the sea the terns, combined with that serene facial expression, immediately start to dismiss the negative preconceptions that so many of us bring to gulls. The job is completed by their liking for genuinely marine habitats – they're most often seen gliding effortlessly over sea-cliffs or skimming the waves, and they lack the predilection for easy pickings shared by all those individuals of the above-mentioned species who do make their homes by the sea. Not for them the sort of carefully planned and ruthlessly executed heist carried out by a herring gull against my then girlfriend one summer's day fifteen years ago, when it snatched half a large piece of cod out of her hands within thirty seconds of us leaving the chip shop in Llandudno. We'd probably have considered the cackling calls of the gull's mates, as they applauded his audacity and demanded a share of the spoils, a final withering insult, but in truth we were already pretty withered by the price of the fish and chips.

At all times, and in all locations, kittiwakes seem not so much shy of humankind as completely oblivious to us, making them less familiar than the rest of their family even to many regular birdwatchers, and also giving them that air of genuine wildness. A few are seen inland as they migrate back to their breeding sites, or are blown off course by gales, but for the most part they're strictly maritime birds. Pelagic birds, in fact, to use the correct term for creatures that spend large parts of their lives wandering the seas.

But that seeming aloofness doesn't give entirely the right impression. In their own way, they've been every bit as willing to interact with humans, to their own benefit, as their bolder, louder and more visible relatives; and in turn have been exploited by us to a sometimes horrifying extent. They'll follow fishing boats, for example, to scavenge discards and offal, while as late as the 1950s large numbers of their eggs were harvested for eating. In the middle years of the nineteenth century, as many as five hundred a day per person were shot for 'sport' by Victorian holidaymakers, and worst of all their wings were also used in hats, often being cut off while the birds were still alive.

Perhaps the fact that they no longer have any perceived monetary or culinary value to us is what has allowed them to slip beneath the radar in recent decades, but there's a downside to that relative anonymity, too – one that their entire history in Newcastle encapsulates.

My own fascination with kittiwakes started a long time ago. A modern-day student would probably be horrified at just how un-savvy I was about courses and career options, but back in the late 1980s I based my choice of university on three rather spurious criteria – the social life on offer, the proximity to open country and the birds that would go with it, and the fact that one of the student residences, Leazes Terrace, looked directly into Newcastle United's St James's Park ground.

When I was invited up to Newcastle for a university open day, I discovered there was a lot more to the city than news reports on the decline of shipbuilding and other heavy industry, and repeats of *Whatever Happened to the Likely Lads?* had hitherto revealed. Even a cursory wander through the streets revealed Roman walls, magnificent Georgian terraces sweeping down to the river, the iconic Tyne and High Level Bridges, and below them a bustling quayside dominated on the Gateshead side by the great square bulk of the old Baltic Flour Mills. Being a landlubber born and bred, that merest hint of the ocean ten miles away, and beyond that the bleak but romantic Baltic, was enough to make my mind up. I worked hard to get the necessary grades, and by October was heading up the Great North Road.

I loved Newcastle from the start, but in truth I rarely got as far as the Quayside during my first year. All the inevitable distractions of student life, of which academic work was generally the least, conspired to keep me at the other end of town, around the university itself and the halls at Castle Leazes, which did have the great attraction for a birdwatcher of being surrounded by the rough grassland of Leazes Moor. I didn't let on to any of my friends at the time, of course, but seeing a wheatear standing atop a cowpat there one March morning was one of the highlights of that year (I'm not sure if that reveals just what a staid and uneventful student life I actually led, but try not to judge me).

When I did get down to the Quayside, it was always after dark, usually to visit The Cooperage and its Friday-night disco. Occasionally, there was a Monday-night expedition to the North Sea ferry that had been moored on the Gateshead bank and converted into a nightclub called Tuxedo Junction (imaginatively known as The Boat by all and sundry). But that was it.

Then, one weekend in May, I found myself at a loose end. All my friends, even the most casual drinking acquaintances, had gone home to revise or were locked in their rooms, refusing to be distracted from their work. My own exams were almost over, and I'd had as much of Gregory of Tours as I could stand for one day, so I set out walking under heavy overcast skies. It was Sunday morning, so all the usual stops in town – HMV, Windows music store and the like – were out of the question, and eventually I made my way down one of the steep stairways near the castle.

Almost as soon as I walked onto the Quayside, I was aware of dozens of gulls swirling and scything through the air in front of me. There was nothing especially startling about that – Black-headeds were a familiar sight pretty much everywhere in the city – but it was immediately clear that these were something else. Their ink-dipped wingtips rang a bell, but before I had a chance to ransack my brain for the contents of umpteen half-remembered field guides, the birds themselves considerately provided a huge clue with their calls, a sound straight out of the wild, open spaces of the ocean if ever I'd heard one. Transcriptions of bird songs and calls are notoriously prone to personal interpretations – I've never been able to hear the yellowhammer's 'little-bit-of-bread-and-no-cheese', for example – but it didn't take any great effort to stretch the noise they were making into 'kittiwake'.

I didn't have any binoculars with me – the people in Newcastle were friendly enough, and admirably tolerant of students, but I thought wearing a pair through town would have been testing their acceptance a bit too much. Even with the naked eye, however, I was able to appreciate the kittiwakes' quiet, understated beauty, and to realise that they were all moving to and from the Baltic Flour Mills. Now and then, one or two would land on the water for a few moments, before taking off again and joining the others in their circling flights.

This monolithic reminder of the Tyne's commercial past, built in the 1930s by Hovis, had effectively become a vast kittiwake apartment block, with their nests lining the ledges and alcoves of the towering frontage. The birds wheeled and dipped above the Tyne, and maybe one or two plucked a morsel or two from the surface of the water, but for the most part they must have been arriving from the North Sea with beaks crammed with fish and invertebrates for their endlessly hungry and vocal young. Once their load was delivered, they were off again, back to North Shields and beyond.

In the weeks that followed, I tried to find out more. That meant rooting through books in the city library, and I eventually found that the Baltic Flour Mills building was host to the largest inland kittiwake colony in the world, with hundreds of pairs using it. In fact, they rarely nest anywhere away from the coast, and although they have readily adapted to man-made nest sites such as building ledges elsewhere, these are almost invariably on seafronts and harbours.

Now, I've mentioned before that once you've become a birdwatcher you never quite un-become one, and after several years of my obsession being turned down to a very low heat, this was one of those events that kept it at least simmering away on a back-burner. Why, I wondered, had this particular group of kittiwakes decided to embrace the joys of urban life, especially when it entailed a lengthy commute to their main feeding areas every day? If they could, why couldn't kittiwakes everywhere? And why weren't the city fathers making a bigger deal of it?

I'd seen plenty of kittiwakes before, and I saw plenty of others during my university years while on field trips up the Northumberland coast to Holy Island, where I also added species like purple sandpiper and eider to my life-list, the tally that every birder keeps of every bird they've ever seen; but I remember arriving back at my room that day and realising that the pleasure of birdwatching, for me, wasn't about seeing more and more species, but in being constantly surprised by bird behaviour.

That, and the way that the experience could instantly transport you hundreds of miles from where you were standing. Hearing those kittiwake calls, I'd felt myself simultaneously in the midst of one of the country's largest cities, and completely alone amidst the salt spray and howling winds of some northern clifftop. Birds as travellers in time and space: a concept that takes some getting your head around when you're nineteen years old.

I made a point, in the following two springs, of going down to watch the kittiwakes at their city centre colony, but after I'd finished university they quickly slipped my mind. I tried to find jobs in or near Newcastle, failed and moved back to the Midlands, and despite our little circle of friends' constant promises to keep in touch and organise regular reunions, we drifted apart the way university friends do, sending Christmas cards and seeing each other at increasing numbers of weddings, and one heartbreaking funeral.

We managed to meet up in Newcastle a couple of times, I think, but they were alcohol-soaked affairs that allowed no time for surreptitious gull-watching. I passed through the city twice on the train, on both occasions in autumn, and I was sent there on a training course one February. If I'd given them a thought, I'd have imagined the kittiwakes still gliding to and from the Baltic on some easy, endless circle; but life was getting in the way and my mind turned to other things.

Today, I'm driving up to Edinburgh for the Scottish Birdfair, and the Angel of the North has announced that Newcastle lies just over the next hill. In the old days you had to go across one of its city-centre bridges, but now the A1 passes well to the west in a great sweeping curve, and there's no need to come within sight of the iconic 'coathanger' perched between Newcastle and Gateshead. I'm hungry, though, and the attractions of a saveloy and pease pudding stotty cake quite get the better of any desire to push on to my destination.

My progress through town on foot is slow, thanks to frequent stops to survey sites of former glories and embarrassments, so by the time I reach the Quayside I'm starting to think that I really ought to be on my way again. I know to expect a much-changed scene, the result of regeneration of the waterfront, but I'm still not quite prepared for what meets my eyes.

There's the millennium footbridge, for a start, with its 'blinking eye' design. If it doesn't have the historic appeal of Stephenson's double-decker road and rail bridge, or the instantly iconic looks of the Tyne Bridge, it's still – if you'll excuse the pun – as eye-catching as they come.

The old Victorian buildings on the Newcastle side have either gone, replaced by luxury apartment blocks, or been renovated to within an inch of their lives, and are now home to legal and property development firms, as well as more bars and restaurants than even a legendarily convivial city like Newcastle could possibly need.

On the far side of the river, the new Sage Conference Centre is undeniably impressive, with its glittering, mirrored exterior, although its curious shape does give it the unfortunate appearance (from some angles) of a monstrous chrome woodlouse. But just downstream, what's happened to the Baltic Flour Mills building?

The size and shape is the same as ever, give or take a few air-con vents and external elevator shafts, but the lines of its exterior look cleaner and smoother, and indeed large parts of the brickwork have been totally replaced with glass. This is all entirely in keeping with its new role as the Baltic Centre for the Contemporary Arts, of course, but even without any closer inspection it's obvious that it's no longer a des res for a kittiwake. My heart sinks.

Only for a moment, though, and then it's soaring skywards faster than the snow-white spectre that floats past not ten feet ahead of me. Followed by another, and another, and another, all unmistakable with those black wingtips, and all utterly unconcerned by the dozens of people enjoying the sunshine or the cars humming up and down the road. They don't need to announce themselves for my benefit this time, but they do, again and again.

When the Baltic got its facelift, plenty of thought was given to providing an alternative site for the kittiwakes to nest on, with a special tower being built at a nearby nature reserve on the south bank. It's been well used in recent years, with hundreds of 'tarrocks' (the old fisherman's name for a young kittiwake) being raised there, but the great bulk of the Baltic colony, as many as five hundred pairs, simply moved to the many old stone buildings along the Newcastle Quayside, and to the Tyne Bridge itself. Not only does the great metal arch itself provide numerous nooks and crannies into which a bird can cram a nest, but the two stone towers rearing up at either end of its span offer dozens more.

All of which means that these extraordinary birds are city-centre gulls more than they ever were. Rush-hour traffic passes by nose to tail just a few feet from where the kittiwakes huddle on their nests; and students and other revellers heading for whatever's replaced The Boat stagger past without realising that a quick look over the parapet would bring them face to face with truly wild creatures that might have spent the winter somewhere off the coast of Newfoundland.

In one sense it's a missed opportunity for all those passers-by, because nowhere in these islands is it easier to see a seabird colony at close quarters, but in another it's a relief, because the bridge does at least belong to the council, who can be persuaded (albeit sometimes with extreme difficulty) by the lobbying power and potential electoral might of hundreds of wildlife-lovers not to move the birds on. Private landlords, it's safe to say, generally take a much less lenient view of the birds because of the noise they make, and the inevitable evidence of their presence that they leave streaked all over their chosen home – and the gentrification of this part of the city has only served to increase pressure from this quarter.

But this time, maybe, the birds might just have found somewhere to stay. Information boards now tell their story to visitors, with the hope that they'll eventually become as much an icon of the city as the bridge itself, and slowly but surely Geordies are coming to realise just what a unique natural phenomenon they have in their midst, and what might be lost all too easily. There are even children's picture books celebrating them – give me a child until he is seven, and I will give you the birdwatcher, as an ornithologically inclined version of Ignatius Loyola might have said.

Kittiwakes everywhere are under threat, however; their numbers much reduced by a lack of natural food, caused by overfishing and perhaps the effects of climate change, and even at the best of times the vast colonies that make them Britain's most numerous gull tend to be in places that aren't easily reached.

So next time you're passing through Newcastle in spring or summer, take half an hour to park and walk along the waterfront, look up, and appreciate a unique spectacle, while perhaps reminding the great and good of the city that regeneration and new beginnings don't start and end with humankind. Nowhere, and I mean nowhere, else in the world is all the hi-tech glitter, glamour and grime of the modern urban world carried away quite so effortlessly on the wings of the humble seagull.

6   Living in the City

There's nothing in the world quite so simultaneously disorientating and yet exhilarating as losing all sense of scale and place, of forgetting your own size and shape within the universe. Everything, for a few short seconds at least, becomes unknown and conditional; yet everything also becomes ready to be learned afresh. Everything becomes possible.

I experience it today for a split-second upon waking in a strange hotel bedroom, until the complimentary tea-making facilities come into focus, and the day takes shape before me.

There was also the time when, as a student, I joined the university parachuting club, because I thought its social evenings would be a chance to spend time with a girl with whom I was besotted, and who was also a member. That plan failed dismally, but I stuck at it long enough to make my first jump, at RAF Topcliffe in North Yorkshire, on a gloriously sunny Sunday in early March. I surprised myself by coping well with actually leaving the plane – the jolt and whoosh of air as the static line pulled me upright and opened my chute were similar to the experience of being pushed in at the deep end of a swimming pool when you don't expect it, and certainly no worse.

But what followed remains seared on my memory. First, there was the sensation of standing in mid-air, seeing what felt like the whole of God's Own County flattening out below me, just like smoothing a map on a table. Looking around, I could see the White Horse on the Hambleton Hills, and the North

York Moors beyond, the green, garrison-studded flatlands of the Vale of York, the towers of York Minster to the south, and somewhere behind them the cooling towers at Ferrybridge, the great sprawl of Leeds and Bradford. All of this felt close enough to reach out and touch, as though a step or two in any direction would take me to the edge of the known world. I remember thinking that this is how an eagle must feel.

For the jump we'd been fitted with radio packs that allowed us to listen to instructors on the ground, and suddenly mine crackled into life, telling me to steer towards the instructor's car, parked on one of the runways. I was baffled. I checked, again and again, until the dizzying effect of looking down started to make me feel sick, but I couldn't see any car. The runways were empty. The whole airfield seemed deserted, in fact.

And then, at maybe 400 feet up, the realisation hit me. In my line of vision was what I'd taken to be a red crisp packet. Now, greater proximity and a slight change of perspective gave it new shape, a new identity. It was the Citroën 2CV the instructor had been talking about. I pulled down on my right toggle to steer a little to one side of it, and in what seemed like no time the ground came rushing up and I was bending my knees to take the impact exactly as we'd been taught.

For days, weeks afterwards, I walked around feeling as though I'd had a glimpse into another dimension. It wasn't the weightlessness of standing on the breeze, so much as those moments when I'd been a colossus, able to encompass an entire world within my gaze. Even now, I can close my eyes and find myself back there.

But today, just one hour and three hurried cups of tea after waking up disorientated in the hotel, I'm face to face with something even more dizzying. It's not the pitching and swaying of the boat I'm sitting in, although that doesn't help.

It's not the wind, which, when it gathers its strength and gusts, threatens to take the breath away, literally, forcing my tongue back down my throat. No, it's what appears, at first glance, to be a swarm of flies orbiting the bleached bones of some great sea beast.

The smell is hardly better than you'd expect to find around a carcass, too. There's a distinctively fishy top note, with an ammoniac finish, and an overall miasma of something dredged up from the depths of the wildest oceans.

And then, in the trough between two great swells, in the lull between two great gouts of gale, in a few seconds of cool, calm consideration of what I'm here to see, and do, the buzzing, spiralling insects sharpen into focus, become white crosses that glitter in the thin sunshine and expand and contract as they twist and turn. All at once the world expands to its usual size, or else I shrink.

These are gannets, one of Britain's most unusual and most spectacular birds. It's also a species we have an awful lot of, if you know where to look.

After disembarking, I stand for a moment and try to take in the scale of it all. A seabird city might be the single best reason in the whole of the natural world to stand, head craned skywards and open-mouthed. For other reasons, which the streaked, white hue of the Rock makes obvious, it's the worst reason too.

With a drop in the wind comes the sound: a raucous, insistently grating noise raised by thousands of voices at once, which swells and fades, swells and fades, like waves themselves. This is the song of the rush hour.

Every city has its rush hour, after all. As with any major metropolis, its presence could have been guessed at miles away, even when it was out of sight in an early morning sea mist, due to the steadily gathering volumes of traffic heading to and from its bustling heart. And here, on the edge of downtown, so to speak, there's a constant flow of birds eager to be about the main business of the day, catching fish and bringing them back to their young waiting on the craggy, precipitous, guano-whitewashed rock above.

They've been waiting, you might say, a very long time. Or rather, their kind have. This is the Bass Rock, sitting in the Firth of Forth between the Lothian shore and the ancient kingdom of Fife. It plays host to one of the largest gannetries in the world, a gloriously noisy, smelly, high-rise community that contains as many as 150,000 birds each year, and so closely are bird and site associated that the species' scientific name *Morus bassanus* makes reference to the location.

In the Anglo-Saxon poem 'The Seafarer', which survives in a tenth-century manuscript but is almost certainly at least a couple of hundred years older, there's a wealth of description that sounds like it might be referring to the Bass Rock:

> Hwilum ylfete song
> dyde ic me to gomene,
> ganetes hleothor
> ond huilpan sweg
> fore hleahtor wera,
> mæw singende
> fore medodrince.
> Stormas þær stanclifu beotan,
> þær him stearn oncwæth
> isigfethera;
> ful oft þæt earn bigeal,
> urigfethra; ...

Which, in modern English, is something like:

> I made the wild swan's song
> my game; sometimes the gannet
> and curlew would cry out
> though elsewhere men were laughing;
> and the sea-mew would sing
> though elsewhere men drank mead.
> Storms beat against the stone
> cliffs, and the ice-feathered
> tern called back, and often
> the sea-sprayed eagle too.

'Sea-mew' is a gull, probably the kittiwake, while the eagle, or 'earn', is the white-tailed eagle, now making a comeback in Scotland. And there are echoes of 'huilpan', for curlew, in some Scottish dialect names for the species and the closely related whimbrel – they're still known, in some parts of the country, as whaups.

Certainly the ornithologist James Fisher (1912–1970) thought the Anglo-Saxon poet was talking about the Rock, even arguing that the mixture of species included tied the description to the last ten days of April. Well, maybe, although perhaps we shouldn't forget that poetic licence was just as likely to be indulged in the mead-halls of the Dark Ages as in any modern creative writing workshop.

The ancient reminder of those other species is relevant even today, however, because it's all too easy to become so enamoured of the gannets that you forget the other avian marvels all around you.

There are auks – razorbills, guillemots, and of course puffins. There are gulls, predominantly kittiwakes. And there are fulmars, members of a family – the tubenoses – that ranges from albatrosses, with some of the largest wingspans on earth, to storm-petrels, starling-sized birds that look too frail to survive even a good shower, but which range across the waves every bit as widely as their larger relatives.

Once ashore, I walk up through the gannet colonies with a mixture of fellow birders, more general tourists, and our boat's captain. These birds are remarkably tolerant of man, perhaps because they've learned they have little, directly at least, to fear from us these days. Or perhaps they've always been exactly this way; the huge scale of the harvesting of the birds and their eggs that took place at so many British colonies wouldn't have been possible had they not been so willing to allow a close approach. One or two lunge at our ankles now as we walk up towards the top of the rock, but for the most part they ignore us as we pass.

From the top, we can see the whole expanse of this remarkable seabird city, and even the way that it develops its own neighbourhoods: the oldest, most experienced, most dominant birds are in the city centre, while the younger and less experienced birds find themselves in the windier, wetter, more dangerously exposed suburbs.

And further afield we can see the endless flow of birds to and from the Rock. It's a windy day, so more gannets than usual are skimming the waves like shearwaters or albatrosses, perhaps looking for prey just below the surface, but more likely scanning for food scraps or by-catch from passing ships and boats, or else making the long commute to a preferred feeding ground. If it were stiller, they'd be circling higher, riding the thermals as they spied out feeding opportunities.

These can be a great distance away. When I visited the colony at Les Étacs on Alderney recently I was told that the gannets there range not only to closer, obvious fishing grounds in the Bay of Mont St Michel, and along the Brittany and Normandy coasts, but right back across the Channel, to the waters off Devon and Dorset, and even round into the Thames estuary and North Sea. In this respect, their cities are the opposite of the typical human equivalents. Where ours have become, increasingly, places of commerce and industry, with people living on the outskirts or beyond and travelling in to them, the gannets live in the inner city, enjoying all the advantages of a tight-knit community, commuting each day to their places of work in the wide blue yonder.

Here and there, as we watch, one or two are busy doing the things that we know gannets do, but which make them unlike any other British bird (they're actually closely related to the more exotic boobies). Gaining height, they wait until a glimpse of silver trips a switch and then folds them into a sleek harpoon, plunging into the waves from around thirty feet, at nearly 60 mph.

They don't dive that deep – anything up to fifteen feet – and they're rarely submerged for long, but it's still a remarkable sight, and one that induces an involuntary wince in the observer, until you finally become convinced that their anatomical peculiarities are capable of absorbing the impact with no ill-effects. They have a particularly strong sternum, for a start, and no external nostrils, as well as a layer of fat and dense feather down, while highly developed lungs and air sacs all over their bodies help regulate buoyancy as required.

And if every dive is enough to draw a small, nearly silent gasp of admiration, occasionally you get really lucky – just as the gannets do when one of them spots a dense shoal of fish just below the surface. Then, every bird in the air seems to hang for a moment, quivering with instinct and hunger, before falling like an unexpected strange spring blizzard on the churning, seething waters.

One of the greatest pleasures of visiting Britain's seabird cities is that, much of the time, this also means visiting Britain's many islands. There are mainland colonies, but by their very nature island breeding sites tend to fare better and so grow larger, both because they encounter less direct disturbance from humans, and because the sea acts as a moat, keeping out unwelcome invaders such as rats and cats.

Scotland and Wales boast many of these island colonies. As well as the Bass Rock, there's Ailsa Craig, near the entrance to the Firth of Clyde, Papa Westray in the Orkneys, the Pembrokeshire islands of Skokholm, Skomer and Ramsey, and, taking things to an extreme, the lonely archipelago of St Kilda, forty miles beyond the outermost Outer Hebrides.

When St Kilda was inhabited, until 1930, the population's very survival depended on a systematic but sustainable exploitation of the seabirds, which were used not only as food, but as fuel, too, the fat on the young gannets being utilised in lamps and candles.

Not all these island homes are so difficult to get to. Holy Island, in North Wales, stands barely separated from the main body of the larger island of Anglesey. You can slip across to it without realising, watch the ferries leaving Holyhead harbour on their way to Ireland, then turn your attention to the seabirds of South Stack, which include black guillemots, a dapper but scarcer relative of the more common guillemot. Or there's Rathlin Island, half-a-dozen miles off the Antrim coast in Northern Ireland. It's where a particularly indefatigable arachnid is said to have inspired Robert the Bruce, who was on the run and sheltering in a cave, to continue his struggle to win the crown of Scotland, and when you visit the island you can well imagine that the story is true. When Islay and the Mull of Kintyre loom across the water blue and beautiful on a bright morning, seemingly close enough to reach out and touch, you can understand his reluctance to give them up.

The ferry crossing to Rathlin is quick and easy, and the island has places to stay, and to eat, but best of all it has a uniquely accessible point from which to watch the nesting seabirds. You can cycle up the gentle hills to the West Point, where the RSPB reserve incorporates the lighthouse, enabling you to get right down into the middle of the bickering birds. If it lacks the numbers of some sites, it makes up for that with a rare immediacy and closeness.

In addition to the aforementioned isolation from potential predators, what these islands all have in common, of course, is a variety of habitat perfect for the different species. Across them all, the broader bare ledges relatively low down on the cliffs are preferred by razorbills and black guillemots; both will also nest among boulders, while common guillemots look for narrower but still bare ledges. The eggs of all these species are tapered, to prevent them rolling off, but in all cases it's impossible not to look at them and marvel at the knife-edge existence these birds lead, with eggs and young always only a few inches from oblivion.

Further up the cliffs, on grassier ledges and mini-plateaus, you'll find the gannets and kittiwakes and fulmars, as well as those gulls that haven't decided a suburban life is for them.

Finally, in burrows in the clifftop turf, there are puffins. Along with the kingfisher and the barn owl, they seem to inspire instant and undying affection, even among those casual birdwatchers who have never seen them in the flesh. And while the popularity of those other two species is based on elusive, transient, iridescent beauty, and serene, ethereal grace respectively, the puffin's is rooted in deeply anthropomorphic impulses. It's impossible to see them waddling around their colonies with a rolling sailor's gait, chuntering to each other, without thinking of them as human – and the rather clown-like effect of their large, colourful bills only adds to the effect.

Perhaps there's even more to it than that. Does the puffins' need to live in such close proximity to each other also strike a chord with social animals such as ourselves? There are times, probably, when even the most sociable and convivial of us find ourselves agreeing with Jean-Paul Sartre's claim that 'hell is other people', but not many of us would care to take it to its logical conclusion and put ourselves beyond all human contact. In that respect, we're all puffins and gannets and fulmars and guillemots. Yet seabird cities can often feel so hopelessly crowded that you wonder why there's not even more conflict and aggression than there is; and yet the birds seem to find a way to coexist through a mixture of unwritten rules (handed down who knows how?), ad hoc negotiation, and good old-fashioned muddling through.

They weren't always so densely populated, though, and one of Britain's best seabird breeding sites is a constant reminder of that fact.

Seventh-century Northumbria isn't the obvious place to look for Britain's first wildlife protection laws, but the so-called Dark Ages were nothing like as unenlightened as some would have us believe. Northumbria was one of the largest, and most powerful, of the Anglo-Saxon kingdoms to develop across what's now England after the departure of the Romans. The Celtic-speaking Britons had, for the most part, retreated towards the west and north of Britain, although the picture remained more complicated than that for a long time.

Intermarriage between Celt and Anglo-Saxon was probably fairly common at all levels of society; Celtic political units (such as Elmet, a kingdom around the Leeds area) survived in the heart of 'enemy' territory; and, above all, Christianity provided a certain amount of common ground.

The Germanic settlers encountered this new religion through contact with the Continent: Aethelbert, King of Kent, for example, married a Christian Frankish princess and was then persuaded to accept missionaries from Rome. However, further north the English were converted by Irish missionaries travelling south from what's now Scotland, and the result was a particular kind of Christianity that took much of its inspiration from the 'desert fathers' – hermits, ascetics and monks of the early Church in Egypt. Often this resulted in the practice of *perigrinatio pro Christo*, literally 'exile in Christ', in which the believer undertook to live away from their homeland while they awaited the kingdom of God. Even if the believer stayed closer to home, however, they could strive to become closer to God by living as a hermit.

I'm remembering all this – the content of half-a-dozen essays during my university years – as our boat butts its way through heaving waves towards the Farne Islands, my visit to the Bass Rock having whetted my appetite for offshore exploration. Just a few miles off the Northumberland coast and not far north of Newcastle, these rocky islets figured high in my consciousness throughout my student career. If I wasn't thinking of their seabirds, I was pondering the remarkable life of St Cuthbert.

Growing up near Melrose, St Cuthbert became a monk after seeing a vision on the night that St Aidan, founder of the monastery at Lindisfarne, died. After eventually becoming prior of Lindisfarne himself, and making a name as a humble and tireless evangelist and champion of the poor, he retired to Inner Farne to pursue a contemplative life. Presumably, in his many years criss-crossing Northumbria (which included most of the land between the Humber and the Forth), Cuthbert had already become well acquainted with the bird and mammal life of this sometimes harsh but always beautiful region. It was once he was on Inner Farne that his relationship with the natural world really took off.

For starters, according to the legends, otters were wont to swim over to Inner Farne and use their fur and breath to dry his feet. And then there were the ravens: after the saint had scolded and banished a group of them for stealing straw from the roof of a house that Cuthbert kept ready for guests, one of the corvids returned to beg his pardon, proffering a gift of pig lard as recompense. Cuthbert accepted and the fat was used by his visitors to waterproof their shoes.

Now, both those stories sound like the sort of tall tales that routinely appeared in the saints' lives and hagiographies of the medieval period; the writers (in Cuthbert's case, an anonymous scribe, and then later, a life by the Venerable Bede) were at pains to show that their subject was capable of miracles and all-round holiness.

But the raven story isn't entirely beyond the realms of possibility: recently there was a widely reported story about a girl who received a stream of gifts from the crows she regularly fed. Strip out the details of the cause and effect, and you have what could be a genuine incident involving a species that can still be seen around the Farnes to this day.

What's certain is that Cuthbert had a great concern for, and love of, the natural world. This led, in 676, to his passing special laws to protect the seabirds nesting on the island – in particular the eider ducks, seagoing birds that have, of course, long had a close relationship with man because of our use of their down for bedding. Again, we have to take anything appearing in an early medieval history or saint's life with a healthy pinch of sea salt, but what is inarguable is that to this day eiders are known as 'cuddy ducks' in Northumberland, 'Cuddy' being the locals' affectionate name for the saint.

Striking as they are I'm not here for the eiders today. Nor am I here for the thousands of guillemots and puffins, or even the shags and cormorants perched on the rocks, who look as though they've sprung to life straight from one of the cross-carpet pages of the Lindisfarne Gospels. No, I'm here for what might be the world's greatest avian traveller of all: the Arctic tern.

There are well over a thousand pairs of Arctic terns on the Farnes as a whole, and the reception that they give to visitors can be enough to convince some to turn tail and head back out onto even the choppiest waters. Most birds are willing to risk life and limb to defend their nests and young, and species as disparate as avocets and tawny owls are known for attacking anything that comes too close, but Arctic terns make an art form of it, swooping on intruders, hovering over them, and stabbing away at the tops of heads, or unprotected arms and shoulders. If you've been to the Farnes or a similar colony before, and you've been properly warned, as I have, you know to wear a sturdy hat, at the very least; holding your spotting scope and fully extended tripod in a 'shoulder arms' position can also help deter the worst of the onslaught. Even then you have to accept that a few of these dive-bombers will get through, and if you escape without a scratch your hat and clothes will certainly bear the white-streaked evidence of what you've been through.

But once you have a chance to pause away from the gauntlet of nest-defenders (and many of the nests are right next to the path), the Arctic terns suddenly take on a different appearance and aura, wholly appropriate to the religious past of the islands. As they hover, with the back-lighting sun coming through the translucent primary feathers of their wings, there's something distinctly angelic about them.

Both they and the very similar common tern (a more widespread breeder in the UK, but often found inland) have been known as sea-swallows in the past, thanks to their forked tails and fast, agile flight. But it's the Arctic that is the more deserving of the title – slightly smaller than its relative, there's also something more graceful and elegant about its structure, with its narrower wings and shorter neck. Those primaries help, too; the translucent 'window' on a common tern is smaller and far less noticeable.

Most British breeders can be found in Scotland, and the majority of the wider population are further north still, right up into the Arctic Circle from which the bird takes its name; and yet they spend the northern hemisphere winter in the waters off Antarctica, at the other end of the planet. Recent studies using tracking technology have shown that each bird travels an average of 56,000 miles each year on migration, and one chick from the Farnes, ringed in the nest in 1982, showed up in Melbourne, Australia just three months later, after a journey along the coasts of Europe and Africa, then across the Indian Ocean.

I watch one now, just offshore. Wheeling and gyring, slowing down while it peers into the murky waters, then accelerating sharply away again, it looks like a puppet at times, bouncing on unseen strings. But when it stalls, momentarily, wings outstretched to form a wispy, impressionistic Latin cross, I see it as the creature of light that it is, an unresting pilgrim in constant search of the sun, seeing more hours of daylight every year than virtually any other creature on the planet.

And I wonder what Cuthbert made of it, here alone with only a chattering mass of seabirds for company? He would have known nothing of their long odysseys and their Antipodean sojourns, of course, but perhaps in the regularity of their arrival each spring, and their departure each autumn, he saw a reassuring confirmation of a world working the way that its Creator had meant it to.

Perhaps Cuthbert saw something else, too, in the seabird colonies all around him. Although he'd chosen seclusion in his later years, his had always been a pragmatic Christianity, fully engaged with the material world of the ordinary people, and he can hardly have failed to see, in the seabird cities, the interdependence of the birds.

This manifests itself in many ways. As with bird flocks, there's an element of safety in numbers. Although some studies have shown that the conspicuousness of such colonies also serves to attract predators that might not otherwise notice individual nests, in many cases seabirds can act together to mob intruders and drive them away – as seen in the Farnes. The hatching of chicks in each species is also often synchronised, which means that any predator that does get through is faced with far more prey than it could possibly manage to make off with, and any individual egg or chick has a good chance of surviving.

But there are other reasons, one being that there simply aren't that many suitable nest sites available, given that most seabirds have a very specific habitat requirement. They also need to be within reach of abundant food supplies, although as we've seen with gannets, this can involve a significant commute.

While islands often offer the best combination of conditions for breeding seabirds, there are other places to find them – to the great relief of birdwatchers for whom a boat trip on heaving seas is a sure-fire recipe for a rapid reacquaintance with their breakfast. I'm not, I should add, one of those. I've birdwatched from boats and ships off Iceland, the Falklands, the North Sea, the English Channel and the Mediterranean, in choppy and sometimes downright frightening seas. Not so much as a hint of nausea. But, embarrassingly, I've passed out on a flat-bottomed Thames barge while travelling the perfectly calm waters of the Stour estuary, between Essex and Suffolk; and during a morning's snorkelling in a reef-ringed lagoon off New Britain, Papua New Guinea, I spent most of my time green-faced and bleary-eyed, instead of enjoying the staggeringly beautiful views over textbook South Sea islands and swimming-pool-still waters. The human mind, and the inner ear, are very strange things indeed.

No, in addition to the kittiwakes of the Tyne Bridge, at least one more of the UK's very best seabird cities is visible without ever having to leave dry land, and as I wend my way south from the Farnes, I decide it's high time I made another visit to it. I leave the A1 near Darlington, and head for the coast.

Bempton Cliffs is an RSPB reserve between Flamborough and Filey. When I first came here, maybe fifteen years ago, there wasn't a great deal in the way of facilities at all, but today there's a brand-new visitor centre promising refreshments, a shop, permanent exhibitions, and TV screens relaying live images from the nest sites along the towering cliffs.

Which is all great – anything that helps the casual birdwatcher or nature-lover to connect with these spectacular yet often baffling birds (to an experienced birder, let alone a beginner, seabirds can appear bewilderingly similar, and hopelessly remote) has to be a good thing. But what really makes Bempton special hits me before I've left the car park.

There's another reason why a strong stomach is a good idea if you're going in search of seabird cities, and that's the fact that you can often smell them long before you see them. Indeed, in a fog-bound Scottish firth or sea loch, you can imagine that the overwhelming stench of guano combined with the clamour of thousands of birds is every bit as effective a warning of land full ahead as any lighthouse or foghorn. Most of us find bird excrement little more than an annoyance when dropped onto a freshly washed car or window. Even when we get bespattered ourselves, we tell ourselves that it's good luck (a slightly odd concept, admittedly), but perhaps that's because the average splash of the white stuff doesn't smell of much. In a seabird colony, though, it most certainly does.

In the nineteenth century, guano was big business, being used to produce gunpowder and as a soil fertiliser. Although this mainly came from warmer, drier parts of the globe, such as Peru, where deposits deep enough to require actual mining built up over centuries, it was also taken from colonies closer to home. And this was far from the only way in which seabird colonies were exploited. The eggs of gulls and other species were taken, and the birds themselves, too, were often a source of food – and not just for the poor. Gannets don't, I'd have to say, sound the most appetising of fare, neither fish nor fowl, exactly, but once upon a time they turned up on the menus of Scottish kings, so presumably the distinctly piscine taste wasn't foul, either. In the Second World War there was even an attempt to market them as 'highland geese', although it's hard to find many people who remember them fondly.

Today, however, the gannets, razorbills, guillemots and fulmars of Bempton are safe enough from human depredations, except that our overfishing of the oceans has made food difficult to find for some species, while global warming might also be forcing prey, and the birds with it, further and further north.

As I watch a distant dot tack its way across the waves, before finally resolving into another gannet, perhaps with a crop of half-digested fish for its young, I realise these birds are far too easy for us to co-opt as metaphors; the way their lives appear balanced delicately between earth-bound, sociable domesticity and restless, solitary searching continues to make them favourites of poets and other writers. But – and yes, this is rich coming from someone who has written his fair share of seabird poems – they deserve our attention for no other reason than that they are themselves, and that they're here in these islands in greater numbers than in most places on earth. Until you know our seabirds, you can't know Britain.

7   Killer in Our Midst

It's a day of rich pickings, where the feral pigeons are concerned. Blue skies and hot sun have brought the crowds out, and the whole embankment is thronged with tourists gazing at one of the world's most famous skylines, with office workers on their lunch breaks enjoying the weather, and street traders and performers eager to sell their wares and talents, and no doubt a few locals wondering what happened to what, thirty or forty years ago, was an unfashionable, rather industrial area of south London.

Where there are crowds, of course, there's food – muffins from the coffee stand, doughnuts from a van, burgers from a nearby outlet of a certain international franchise, and salt beef sandwiches from Borough Market. All being enjoyed by the crowds, and all generating a veritable feast of crumbs and morsels and leavings.

If you're not too fussy about your diet (what pigeon is?) and take a fairly liberal approach to food hygiene (as pigeons generally do), then today you can eat very well indeed. Perhaps forty pigeons are scattered around the concourse of the Tate Modern art gallery, formerly the Bankside power station, dodging nimbly between the feet of hurrying people to give the lie to their rather portly appearance. Here and there, they're joined by the odd house sparrow, that most emblematic of London birds, and on the path along the embankment, a couple of black-headed gulls also come to the buffet, swooping to snatch the remains of a dropped takeaway meal.

But it's the pigeons that do most of the dining. They tend not to inspire a great deal of affection or even tolerance in the hearts of birdwatchers or more casual observers, with 'sky-rat' being one of the more printable epithets thrown their way, but they shrug off such abuse the same way they do the pollution of the great, grimy city. Generation after generation have made the capital their home, congregating at every major tourist spot to take advantage of the endless opportunities on offer, like so many avian Del Boys. I have a photo of my own parents in Trafalgar Square, in the early 1960s, surrounded and covered by pigeons.

A clue to one of the reasons why birders dismiss them so willingly can be found in the first part of their name – feral. As in formerly domestic, now 'gone wild' again, but betraying their tame past not only in their habits, but in their endless variety of colours and markings.

A few, at least, retain the look of their forebears: the rock doves that once nested on sea cliffs and mountain crags long before man came into the picture. And which still nest there in a few locations on the furthest northern and western edges of Great Britain and Ireland. These birds are a neat mixture of greys and purplish-blues, with a startlingly white rump that only reveals their exact identity as they flee at high speed.

For some of their city lookalikes years of urban living have taken the edge off the flying skills and swiftness associated with their ancestors. A diet of exclusively fast food is no better for a pigeon than for a person. And it has made them complacent, too. Because, many centuries after they made the move into the urban landscape, their most deadly ancestral enemy has also embraced an environment of high-rise blocks and man-made canyons, of twenty-four-hour living by the light of neon and halogen – and the pigeons are item number one on its menu.

Three pigeons circle now, just about at the level of the tops of the gallery's towers. I watch them through my binoculars, and high above and beyond them another shape comes into view, itself rather pigeon-chested, but with a long tail and pointed wings held slightly flexed at the carpal joint as it powers its way a little higher with shallow wingbeats.

It's not, in itself, the most immediately impressive bird in flight, but even now it has the air of something completely different, and within seconds it is transformed totally. The wingbeats quicken, the flight becomes more purposeful, and then it folds into itself and drops for all the world as though shot dead.

A couple of hundred feet below it, but still a long way above the ground, the third pigeon, a little plumper and slower than the other two, and a touch more conspicuous with its brown and white mottled plumage, doesn't know what's about to hit it. Even were it to look up, the hunter is coming straight out of the sun, in classic Battle of Britain style, and travelling at around 200 mph, so escape would be highly unlikely. Powerful talons, balled into fists, strike the pigeon in the back of the neck, breaking it instantly. The force of the impact sends its wings and tail fanning and flaring out, acting like a parachute to slow its head-over-heels fall towards the ground. But long before it reaches terra firma, the killer has circled down and round, grabbing the pigeon's corpse firmly; and then there follow the same shallow, almost lazy wingbeats as earlier, carrying its prize away to a ledge on the highest tower.

The peregrine is back, and no pigeon will ever be safe again.

It's easy, now, to forget just what a resurrection this bird has undergone, both in actual, physical terms, and in the consciousness of the public. Like most raptors, it had always suffered a certain amount of persecution from gamekeepers and shooting interests, and has never been a popular bird with pigeon-fanciers, but population levels remained at a sustainable level until the species was hit by a double-whammy.

First of these was the Second World War. Six years of bloody, tragic conflict actually had beneficial effects for some British birds: avocets recolonised the areas of coastal East Anglia that had been flooded as a defence against German invasion, while the bomb-sites of the Blitz provided a mock-montane environment that allowed the black redstart to get a foothold in this country. Peregrines, on the other hand, were enemies of the state. The Special Operations Executive used messenger pigeons on a massive scale to carry messages back to Britain from occupied Europe, and the last thing needed was for vital information to end up in a falcon's stomach, so the peregrines of southern and eastern England were harried as mercilessly as the Wehrmacht.

Just as the bird began to recover ground a little in the aftermath of VE Day, along came a new generation of pesticides, such as DDT. These chemical substances played their part in boosting agricultural production, of course, and were welcomed by a nation suffering from austerity, but as the years went on it became clear that something was badly wrong. The pesticides had found their way into the food chain and worked their way to the top – which meant that raptors such as the peregrine and the sparrowhawk didn't stand a chance. Rather than being directly poisoned, these birds suffered year after year of breeding disasters, with the chemicals thinning their eggs to the extent that they were easily broken by incubating females.

By the early 1960s, the peregrine was desperately threatened in Britain. At this time, along came an Essex librarian by the name of J.A. Baker, a keen but far from expert birdwatcher who enjoyed recording the avian life he saw near his Chelmsford home. On the face of it, his book *The Peregrine* is simply an account of his wanderings during the harsh winter of 1963, following the falcons on the estuaries and saltmarshes of the area.

If you've fallen under its spell, however – and I count myself among the growing band who have – it's perhaps the most extraordinary piece of sustained nature writing in the English language, a virtuoso prose poem that acts as an elegy for a bird on the brink of disappearing, as well as a supreme evocation of the English winter. Baker's writing is so intense, so concentrated with the essence of all that is wild, that you find yourself only able to sip at it, like a fifty-year-old single malt. If you intend to read it, and you should, put aside plenty of time.

Intriguingly, recent research by Conor Jameson, author of *Looking for the Goshawk* and *Silent Spring Revisited*, suggests that at least a few of the 'peregrines' Baker watched were misidentified by him, perhaps confused with some falconers' hybrids among them; and also that some of the behaviour he mentions was a direct result of the pesticide-poisoning. But as Jameson says, these considerations don't for a moment take away from the enduring impact of a truly unique book: Baker reminded us, in timely fashion, of exactly what we were about to lose, and added an extra layer of glamour, in the original, magical sense of the word, to a bird that already figured high in the imagination of every birdwatcher.

It would be great to be able to say that Baker's masterpiece was one of the books that fired the enthusiasm of this nascent birdwatcher, but the truth is a little less romantic. It also, as you've probably come to expect, involved the *Reader's Digest*.

My parents both being teachers, I was lucky enough to grow up in a house in which books were never in short supply, although neither my mother nor my father was a voracious consumer of fiction. Other than some nineteenth-century classics, most of the novels in our house belonged to the *Reader's Digest* Condensed Books series – effectively mini-anthologies containing four or five stripped-down novels. Quite how much they condensed them, I can't say, but I do remember reading Jack Higgins's *The Eagle Has Landed* in this format, then reading the full version years later, and wondering what the difference was. Incidentally, I picked that book up purely because it mentioned birds in the title, and while my brief disappointment was assuaged by the gripping nature of the thriller, I was also quietly satisfied by the setting (the British birdwatching paradise of the north Norfolk coast), and the fact that two of the characters briefly take time out from the action to talk about looking for shore larks.

That same filtering method when looking for potential reading material – first select anything with a bird's name in the title – served me even better when I came across a novel called *In the Shadow of the Falcon*, by Ewan Clarkson, in that condensed book series. This time, the bird was more than a mere codeword for an elaborate attempt to kidnap Winston Churchill, instead being the central character, rather in the style of Henry Williamson's *Tarka the Otter*, or the rabbits in *Watership Down* by Richard Adams. I can't recall exactly how the plot turns out, but I do remember that the pair of peregrines in the book faced many dangers, both natural and man-made, in their bid to raise a family, and I remember being completely enraptured, devouring the story in one sitting with an enthusiasm I had hitherto reserved for the likes of *The Hobbit*. Part of its appeal, I think, was that spotting a peregrine seemed only a tiny bit more likely than stumbling into a hobbit. While the kestrel I regularly watched hovering over the hill behind our house was an exciting, thrilling reminder that the natural world was never far away, its larger, more glamorous relative seemed impossibly unattainable.

There was one slim chance, though. Even in the darkest days, peregrines had hung on in a few of the more remote areas of Britain, such as around our rocky coasts, where prey items were less likely to be farmland birds. Now the novel was set in Pembrokeshire, and when I flicked through our big old atlas of Great Britain (yes, yes, another *Reader's Digest* publication), it looked perfectly plausible to me that there would be peregrines in that county in real life too. I wondered if they might even edge their way east along the coast of South Wales.

I settled on that location specifically because, every summer, we'd spend at least ten days or so down with my grandmother in Bridgend. The beaches and fairground of Porthcawl were distraction enough for a young lad, and could quickly banish any thoughts of Wales as a wild, unspoiled corner of the country, but some days we'd leave town by the other route, and head to Ogmore-by-Sea and Southerndown. Here, even the road looked promising, with steep hills covered with bracken, gorse, and dramatic, rocky outcrops – and the coast itself was perfect. Cliffs, rocky shores, and rising beyond them those hills again. Given all this I rather let my peregrine fixation get the better of me, and convinced myself that if I could only be patient, and vigilant, I'd be rewarded by the sight of one soaring in the sunshine, before dropping onto its unfortunate prey.

I was similarly optimistic, and unrealistic, when it came to another rare raptor. In those days, red kites were one of

Britain's rarest breeding birds, with all field guides describing them as being restricted to the wooded valleys of mid-Wales. Again, a swift look at a road atlas convinced me that this vaguely defined region started a few miles north of the M4, and that were we to head in the direction of Brecon, we'd see the unmistakable long-winged, fork-tailed outline of these graceful carrion-eaters. Once, on a day too drizzly and cool for the beach, we did drive up the valleys to the Bwlch, where the route crossed the mountains, winding its way down beside great rock walls covered in paintings of Welsh dragons and the like. But I only had eyes for the peregrine-nesting potential of the rocky nooks and crannies, and the wide skies to the north of us with the kite-spotting possibilities they offered. The raptors were there, I was sure of that.

I was doomed to disappointment, of course. I hadn't appreciated just how rare (maybe half-a-dozen pairs) the kites were, or how long it can take a species to bounce back and expand its range after years of decline, as with the peregrines. But I learned something about birdwatching, which is that optimism is as vital a part of your kit as binoculars, and in the years that followed I never stopped looking, or hoping.

Nor did a lot of other birders. Peregrines carried on quietly but steadily building up their numbers in their strongholds, until they reached the point at which the young birds had to start roaming further and further afield in search of new territories. The bird's very name, meaning 'wanderer', is a clue to its peripatetic tendencies, and pairs prefer to maintain large territories. For that reason it wasn't long before they started looking at distinctly untypical breeding sites.

Red kites, on the other hand, were given a helping hand by the authorities, the Welsh population having become so small that extinction in the UK was very much on the cards, and with the bird being threatened more generally across its worldwide range. The RSPB had been involved in trying to protect it since 1905, and although they succeeded in reducing illegal poisoning and egg collecting, numbers increased only very slowly, so there was little chance of the bird spreading beyond its Welsh heartland any time soon. That led to the decision, in 1986, to start a reintroduction programme, initially on the Black Isle, near Inverness, and in the Buckinghamshire Chilterns, followed by further releases in Rockingham Forest, Northamptonshire; central Scotland; Dumfries and Galloway; around Harewood House, Leeds; and in the Derwent Valley, near Gateshead. There have been setbacks, for sure, with persecution proving a problem in Scotland, but for the most part the scheme has been a spectacular success, with the releases in intensively farmed southern and central England proving to be the most successful of all.

In most respects, this reflects what was hoped might happen. In many parts of the world, the bird's close relative, the black kite, is a fixture of man-made landscapes, including city centres, where they act as flying waste disposal units that feed on carrion, food waste, and the general detritus of human day-to-day life – not for nothing were they known, in British India, as 'shite-hawks'.

Literature suggests that the red kite filled much the same niche in Britain in the not too distant past. Shakespeare makes more than one reference to the species, using its name as an insult in *King Lear* (presumably because of the negative associations of its carrion-eating), and making reference in *The Winter's Tale* to the bird's curious habit of collecting unusual items, including clothing, for its nest. Both strongly suggest that it was a familiar sight for the mainly urban audience the Bard was writing for.

So, while generations of Britons, including my own, had grown up thinking of the red kite as a bird of one of the wildest, emptiest parts of Britain, in fact, all things being equal, it prefers a gentler, rather less bleak landscape. If that means living cheek by jowl with mankind, then so be it.

The extent to which the kites have embraced that landscape, and the new breeding opportunities afforded to them by a lack of persecution, are brought home to me on the way back from the Tate. I'd normally have taken the train to London, but I need to be at a poetry reading in Birmingham in the evening, and the logistics of getting the train back from there to Leicester late at night are just too daunting. So, after a surprisingly easy escape from the capital and the ever-circling wall of steel that is the M25, I head in my car along the M40 towards the second city.

What happens next shouldn't be a surprise. I've read about it several times, and the RSPB and others are rightly keen to make a big noise about it. Nevertheless, I'm totally unprepared for what an immense emotional punch a now-familiar bird can deliver.

Just where the motorway goes through a cutting around Stokenchurch, a couple of drizzly clouds disappear away to the north, and blue skies and late afternoon sunshine bathe the Chiltern vista. Within a minute the unmistakable shape of a red kite – long wings held crooked at the 'elbow', and long forked tail used as a rudder – appears above the six lanes, and then another, and another, and another, until I can count a dozen without having to take my eyes off the road. As the road starts to descend slightly, and the countryside opens out on either side, I can see that these are just a fraction of the local population – perhaps three times as many are in view in total, soaring and wheeling on the thermals, flapping with a leisurely assurance, and occasionally swooping down to take a closer look at a piece of roadkill, or a rubbish tip, or a discarded takeaway.

What's interesting is that the towns and villages beneath them, their gardens and car parks, their roads and verges and shopping centres, have clearly become every bit as much a part of these birds' natural habitat as any remote Welsh valley. For the kites the former are a vast, ever-replenishing larder, just as the Chilterns escarpment acts as a huge thermally powered elevator that sends them high into the sky with minimum effort, and the spinneys and hangers that dot its slopes are convenient homes and dormitories.

To see this bird, which only a few years ago was emblematic of rarity and remoteness and the fragile state of an entire eco-system, thriving so visibly just a few miles outside one of the world's great cities, was enough to bring a tear to the eye. Of course, not all birds can so readily adapt to the changing circumstances that man forces upon them, but in some cases at least, we're brought up short against the realisation that we really don't know the natural world anything like as well as we think we do.

I end up pulling over at the next service area and spending half an hour watching the kites going about their business. Sometimes in life, you do get exactly what you want. Birdwatching has a pleasant habit of reminding you of that fact.

So it was with peregrines. At some point in the years when I'd left birdwatching (but birdwatching hadn't entirely left me), I read a newspaper article about them nesting in the middle of New York City, with the skyscraper-lined canyons perfectly mimicking their natural habitat. I was entirely out of touch with developments in British ornithology, but I remember wondering whether such things might also happen here, eventually. I rather assumed I'd be an old man before they did.

I was wrong. Before long, there were reports of the birds from a number of British cities, with cathedrals often favoured as nest sites. The spread has continued, and so I find myself in York, at the invitation of *Bird Watching* contributor and friend Paul Brook, to look for the pair that have taken up residence on the famous Minster.

As I meet Paul at the front of the ancient building, a strong, cold wind whips up, and we wonder if we're going to be out of luck. We walk round the corner to the little green, preparing ourselves for disappointment, but have to wait less than a minute to find our target.

The word 'iconic' gets bandied about a lot these days, too often used to describe things that are anything but. On this occasion, however, it's wholly appropriate. Our first sight of the peregrine is of it perched like some heraldic beast on one of the carved stone pinnacles, unmoving as any gargoyle. It's as if the bird is intent on reminding the public of its former status as a bird of kings and noblemen.

Curiously, the nearby pigeons show no fear of their arch-enemy, perching almost close enough to touch the raptor. These peregrines are relative newcomers, so perhaps the pigeons simply don't know the peril they're in yet; or perhaps they're wiser than we think, and know that however deadly a peregrine is in its element of choice – air – perched it is no threat. Neither is it likely to grab another perched bird, in the manner of a goshawk or an eagle owl.

A couple of minutes later, as some of the pigeons are undertaking one of their periodic circular flights around the little park, there's a sudden scattering of the flock, as something dashes through the middle of them at high speed. It makes two or three passes, with enough conviction to induce panic among the pigeons, but without ever seeming to actually want to catch one. When it starts calling to the first, statuesque falcon, we conclude that it's a male, showing off to the icily unimpressed female.

He circles a few times and then heads off across the city, and as he does so I realise that the shape of a peregrine in flight and its style of flying were burned into my memory from a very early age. At primary school we used to watch a programme called *Look and Read*, which showed an ongoing serial. One of the earliest I saw was called *Skyhunter*, and featured children trying to protect a peregrine's nest from egg thieves. At that time, my interest in birds was slowly evolving out of my previous obsession with dinosaurs (appropriately enough, given that scientists now generally agree that birds are, effectively, living dinosaurs), while another keen interest was in planes, sparked by making model kits of Lancaster bombers and Spitfires. In fact, most of what I knew about planes was derived from the huge Airfix catalogue I had. Swing-wing jets were cutting-edge technology, and I remember wondering why none of them were named after the peregrine: to me, its structure and flying style, with the 'arm' seeming to remain still and the 'hand' doing all the work, combined with that blistering speed, of course, were reminiscent of nothing so much as an F-14 or a Tornado.

Back in the present, the male is gone, and the female continues her stony-faced vigil up on the medieval masonry.

We're both aware that we've just enjoyed one of those slices of serendipity that sometimes makes birdwatching seem an implausible melange of luck and coincidence. In fact it involves both, but the more you practise it, the luckier you get (to paraphrase the golfer Gary Player), and just as with playing golf or any other sport, a lot of its appeal lies in the fact that as your abilities and knowledge develop, you notice your own efforts less and less. It's like performing a conjuring trick on yourself, and being taken in every time.

By the time I've driven home, Paul has messaged me on Twitter to say that the peregrines have been seen mating, a first for York, adding the site to a list of locations including Chichester, Derby and Worcester, where the cathedrals have gained new, living statues.

Nests have been protected and monitored (with some projects showing that the raptors take an extraordinary range of prey, even hunting by night with the help of the churches' floodlights), and watch points have been set up at locations such as Tate Modern to give the public a new stake in conserving these remarkable birds.

In the days when I became a birder again in earnest, I restricted most of my watching to a couple of sites near home, both of which were essentially gently rolling countryside. When peregrines crossed my thoughts, which was often, they were shadows darkening the rock walls of half-remembered Welsh mountains, or arrows sent arcing across the skies above distant coastal saltmarshes. During a rare trip to one of the latter, at Titchwell in Norfolk, one did wing its way out of my daydreams and into the real world, flashing high over the pools and reed beds and lifting thousands of geese, ducks and waders in panic as it did so.

I wasn't, at the time, a member of any of the local birding or wildlife groups; nor was I signed up to any of the bird news services that had emerged and which used pagers to send birdwatchers scurrying from one end of Britain to the other in pursuit of their quarry. I wasn't even particularly Internet-savvy. So rumours reached me the way they always had, through conversations in hides, or huddled on the side of drab, grey reservoirs. And from them, I learned that the hard facts of geology had delivered what I'd wanted to witness as a birder ever since I was a child.

Charnwood Forest is an irregular triangle of woods, heathland and high sheep pasture which sits between my house and Leicester on a bed of ancient granite, some of the oldest rocks in Britain. Much in demand as roadstone, the granite has brought a scattering of quarries across the north-west corner of the county, from the vast hole that has consumed half of Bardon Hill, Leicestershire's highest point, to smaller, older workings.

And peregrines had found these quarries, I was told. Their sharp, sheer walls were exactly what the falcons were looking for as they wandered in search of new nest sites. In the case of working quarries, the high security round them meant the birds could raise their young free from the attentions of egg-collectors, photographers and overzealous birdwatchers.

Soon I'd seen my first local peregrine, one of a pair that bred close to a favourite waterside birdwatching spot. Had seen the pair, in fact, sitting on a prominent bare tree on the skyline, surveying their domain with its ample supplies of woodpigeons, ducks and crows. Peregrines, it should be noted, spend a huge amount of time sitting still, both because the large size of their prey makes for a meal that lasts them all day, and because the high-velocity explosion of their hunting routine is not something that can be performed without the right rest and preparation. They are the Usain Bolts of the bird world, finely tuned athletes built for a few seconds of intense activity every few hours.

One summer's evening, they were sitting in the same spot, while a little way beyond them three more falcons tilted and lunged at the swirling swallows and martins. At first, I took these falcons for hobbies, another raptor species that has expanded its range in recent years and which has a predilection for hirundines. But as I looked closer I could see they had the peregrine's powerful build, rather than the rakish elegance of the smaller bird, and realised that their lack of size was down to age. These were the newly fledged young of the pair on the tree, testing their flying skills – unsuccessfully, I should add – against plentiful targets.

In the years that followed, I'd see similar scenes at three other local quarries, including one that I can walk to from home, but the thrill never diminished. If anything, seeing the falcons become part of the place where I'd lived most of my life made the experience even more exciting: every encounter with them was like a brief journey into a parallel existence, a world like our own in almost every respect, but infinitely more thrilling.

The two worlds merge, sometimes. Today, I'm sitting high up behind the goal in the King Power Stadium, home ground of Leicester City. The team has been the object of my affection and obsession for nearly as long as birds have, but have caused me infinitely more disappointment, so my attendance has dwindled to almost nothing in recent years. But I'm with two friends, one of whom is over from his new home in California and is desperate to take advantage of this rare opportunity to see the national game, and it's a bright, sunny day and the visitors are Nottingham Forest, the bitterest of local rivals.

It's a good game, end to end, and we're well into the second half before I notice that there's something sat on the edge of the stand away to the right. I curse the fact that I haven't got any binoculars with me, and the object is so unmoving that I start to wonder whether it's one of the hawk decoys put on buildings to ward off pigeons.

Then it flies. Nothing spectacular, just steady, muscular wingbeats taking it up and beyond the far goalmouth, before it swings round in a wide curve. And every pigeon and black-headed gull within five hundred yards sees it for what it is, and lifts into the air and makes haste to depart the scene, just as 30,000 people jump to their feet to applaud Leicester's well-deserved equaliser. And I leap up too, but I'm not sure whether my roar of joy is directed at the team in blue below me, or the slate-blue assassin that has flown out of a lifetime's dreams into the spring sky above.

8   The World in a Field

I notice them first as I make my way from the bus. Individuals and pairs, walking purposefully in the same direction as me, or pausing on corners for brief, animated discussions which, when overheard, add up to a veritable babel of tongues. It's not long after seven in the morning, and the sun-bathed city streets are still quiet, so their presence and movements are as obvious as those of the pigeons that flock and scatter, flock and scatter, ahead of every car or street-sweeper.

Once I reach the railway station they're everywhere. The ones and twos have agglomerated into larger, noisier groups that wheel and drift across the concourse and the first platform, with a feeling of pent-up energy about to be released. There are cries of recognition. Greetings. Necks are craned, looking for the arrival of the train from Birmingham. When it turns up, a couple of minutes late, I take a seat in the first carriage and continue to watch and listen. English is being spoken in every conceivable accent, from West African to Australian and everything between, but there's Spanish too, Castilian, Latin American and other varieties I don't immediately recognise. Two men in the seat ahead of me chat in what I take to be Dutch. Another voice, a little further away, is unmistakably Scandinavian.

It's when we finally pull to a halt in Oakham and spill onto the little station that the grand scale of this migration is revealed. Perhaps two hundred people clad in a bewildering variety of branded polo shirts and baseball caps, photographers' waistcoats and walking trousers, and carrying everything from expensive DSLR cameras to shooting sticks and umbrellas, spill out of what would, normally, be a quiet commuter train, and join a scattering of similarly attired folk who arrived on the earlier service. Outside, a handful of taxi drivers are striking deals and loading up baggage, while a minibus pulls in and starts embarking a patient queue of passengers. This is Britain, so even though it's August, nearly everyone local is compelled to comment with surprise on the blue skies and hot sunshine above us.

I'm in no hurry, so I walk. If you asked any of the new arrivals for their idea of a typical English town, then the ironstone centre of Oakham, with its market square, castle and dreaming spire, is probably close to what they'd have in mind; and the gently rolling countryside beyond, farmland punctuated by hedges and spinneys, would very likely meet their expectations of the English countryside, too. But the roundabout on the edge of town is the first hint that everything is not exactly as it seems, crowned as it is by the figure of an osprey, wings outstretched, carved from a single piece of wood with a chainsaw. The swirling gulls in the middle distance are another clue.

I turn off the main road, and walk alongside a rapidly growing line of traffic, then turn again onto a narrow lane that's also busy with its fair share of vehicles. The cries of gulls and the unmistakable detuned radio bleeping and whirring of lapwings comes from away to the left, where shallow lagoons are hidden behind an earth bank; but for once bird calls fade into the background of my thoughts, and the distant but resonant booming of a loudspeaker takes their place.

'Ladies and gentlemen, the twenty-fifth British Birdwatching Fair is now open.'

I have a confession to make. Even though I've spent the great bulk of my life living no more than thirty miles from the place, it took me the best part of thirty years to fully cotton on to what an amazing spot Rutland Water is. Worse than that, I harboured a largely irrational prejudice against it for part of that time.

When I was around seven years old, my parents took me and my sisters to visit family friends in Peterborough, the city where I now work. It was a wintry day, and thinking back it may also have been the day I saw my first league football match (Peterborough versus Grimsby, with the home side winning 3–1). But whatever the case, on the way, I remember my dad pointing out the huge new reservoir that had been created in this corner of the East Midlands.

Perhaps the grandness of the name, Rutland Water, created wholly unreasonable expectations, because when I caught sight of it, it looked no more impressive than any old flooded field. Leafless trees stuck up from the murky water here and there, and closer inspection revealed old buildings, fence posts, hedges and telegraph poles as well. Far from being an image of natural beauty, it looked like a scene of post-industrial desolation, or some appalling natural disaster. I turned away and promptly forgot about it for another fifteen years.

Where I was being ludicrously unfair, of course, was in failing to work out that the reservoir would develop and mature. Water levels rose. Those rather sad vestiges of the former valley of the River Gwash disappeared beneath them. The harder edges of the lake were smoothed out, and reeds, bushes and trees soon gave the banks a wholly natural look. Not that everything about the place suggested an unspoiled rural idyll, of course. Car parks and visitor centres sprawled over parts of the shores for those visitors who wanted to walk or cycle around the perimeter, while a sailing club occupied a site on the south arm (the lake is essentially the shape of an elongated horseshoe laid flat, with the Hambleton peninsula separating two arms). Sailing, fishing and general tourism provide owners Anglian Water with valuable extra income, as well as doing their bit to assuage any dissatisfaction from locals upset that their valley has disappeared.

Even so, at a site the size of Rutland Water, it's not that difficult to get away from such activities. There are still plenty of quiet corners if you want them. Two of these peaceful spots were set aside and designated as such right from the outset. Together these areas at Egleton and Lyndon make up the Rutland Water Nature Reserve, with a main visitor centre situated at the former and a rather smaller building at the latter. In the years since their creation they too have matured and developed, until now they form a location of international importance in conservation, especially of wildfowl.

Not many men, these days, get the chance to shape an entire landscape, or at least not for the better. But that's exactly what Tim Appleton has done in his forty years as manager of the Rutland Water Nature Reserve.

He remembers driving past the site even as the lake was being created – it was on his route from Peakirk, near Peterborough, where he worked for the Wildfowl & Wetlands Trust, to his home city of Bristol. He watched as the dam took shape, and the valley started to fill, not thinking that within months he'd be working there. It was a hard decision to move. He loved working at the WWT, but in the end, when the reserve manager's job came up in 1975, the lure of being in at the start of something with such enormous potential was too much to resist.

'No one had done anything on this scale before,' Tim explains. 'I did have something of a vision as to how it would work, and I was given a pretty free rein.'

As he says this he points out of his office window in the Egleton visitor centre. Virtually every tree or decent-sized bush that we can see, with the exception of some distant giants on the hill at Burley, is there as a result of the creation of the reserve, not to mention the lagoons and reed beds that make this anything but your typical reservoir.

'I planted 100,000 trees in the first two years,' he says. 'With the reed beds, I dug twenty-five channels by hand, and then piled in rhizomes from the Burley Fish Ponds. Now we have fourteen hectares of reed bed, with booming bitterns.'

Two things, he says, have made this all possible. One is the massive support he has received from staff and hundreds of volunteers. The other is the way the reservoir as a whole has been managed. Strict zoning policies have enabled conservation and recreation areas to thrive alongside each other, and alongside the lake's day-to-day raison d'être – supplying water to nearby Peterborough.

'The proudest thing about my time here, perhaps,' says Tim, 'is that we have maintained a forty-year partnership with Anglian Water.'

He's right. This is a working reservoir that is a Site of Special Scientific Interest, an internationally recognised RAMSAR site – the designation given to globally important wetlands – and a European Special Protection Area, on account of its wintering populations of ducks such as shoveller and gadwall. As we speak, two of the latter paddle across the lagoon in front of us. They're subtly beautiful birds, easily overlooked in favour of showier ducks, such as the pintails just beyond them; but Rutland Water's story, and more importantly that of the British Birdwatching Fair, is inextricably linked with wildfowl from the start.

Like all the best ideas, Birdfair (as it's known to most birders) was born in a pub, the appropriately named Finch's Arms at Hambleton to be exact, on the peninsula jutting out into the middle of Rutland Water. There, Tim Appleton met with Martin Davies of the RSPB, and the rest is history.

'It all stemmed from the mid-1980s, when we used to stage what we called a wildfowl bonanza here,' says Tim. 'Martin had started working in the area and was an innovative guy, and my mentor had been Sir Peter Scott, whose ethos was very much "birds and people", not conservation with a fence around it.

'The Game Fair was held at Belvoir, and it struck us that there was nothing similar to that kind for birdwatching, even though it was becoming increasingly popular.'

Tim and Martin spoke to optics retailer In Focus, who had already enjoyed some success staging demonstration days, and got them on board; and they in turn secured the support of Swarovski Optik, the new boys on the block in the binocular market at the time, who chipped in £2,000.

'We wanted it to be about places that people could go to, so there was and is an ecotourism bias,' says Tim.

'We made money for conservation right from the start – £10,000 in 1990. It occurred to us to ask how we were going to manage the money, and so BirdLife got on board, too.'

The involvement of BirdLife, the international umbrella organisation that coordinates the conservation efforts of charities and NGOs in well over a hundred countries, was a huge seal of approval for Birdfair, and the catalyst for an expansion that continues to this day. I find myself seeing it like one of those shots from a TV programme, where an aerial camera pans back from its focus on a single house, rapidly taking in first the whole British Isles, then Europe, then the globe. The work and vision of one small division of The Wildlife Trusts – Leicestershire and Rutland is one of the country's more modestly proportioned – was being taken to the rest of the country by the RSPB, and to the rest of the world by BirdLife.

Tim says: 'We thought we could probably do a lot more good with the money abroad – if our own NGOs can't do enough here, we're on a hiding to nothing anyway. And so we've looked overseas, and we've been quite bold, targeting places like Cuba and Myanmar.'

Throughout it all Birdfair has retained a pleasantly homespun feel; for all the talk of it being 'birdwatching's Glastonbury', it has little of the music festival's present-day slickness and in-your-face commercialism.

'For twenty years we never really had a proper budget – we just gave away the money we raised, and started again when the money from stallholders started coming in,' Tim says. 'We have limited expenses, and a great team running it all.'

Nevertheless, there's been a certain amount of carping about the fair on forums and in the under-the-breath chatter you hear around hides, and Tim admits that such criticism hurts. But the real refutation of such nay-sayers comes from Birdfair's success: £14 million raised for conservation, once match-funding and seeding is taken into account, and an ever-increasing itinerary of bird fairs all around the world, all taking the Rutland event as their model. Tim's kept busy visiting them to offer advice, or just to speak at them – at

Doñana in Spain, in Portugal, Colombia, South Africa, Uganda and the United States.

So what has made Birdfair such a success? What is the magic ingredient these far-flung locations seek to emulate?

'We had three goals when we started,' he says. 'First, we wanted to be a shop window for conservation, and conservation organisations and businesses. Secondly, we wanted to bring birders from around the world together.'

They've certainly succeeded in the latter. It's not unusual at Birdfair to see Israelis and Palestinians sharing birding stories, for example. And the third factor?

'Fun! We wanted it to be fun.'

It is fun. It's the fun of being surprised by birds and destinations you didn't know existed (even if, like me, you've been to the last eight or nine Birdfairs), and feeling a sudden, overwhelming longing to see such beauty. It's the fun of learning the smallest details about birds – from the reproductive habits of the bullfinch to the hunting strategies of the Steller's sea eagle – from as celebrated a collection of birdwatchers and ornithologists as you'll ever see gathered together. It's about hearing speakers who have travelled from the other side of the planet – literally, and who pack so much passion, local knowledge and hope for the future into a thirty-minute lecture that you leave enthused, educated and convinced that conservation isn't merely a long, hopeless rearguard action against conspicuous consumption and perpetual growth.

It's about walking through the art marquee, marvelling at the huge hold birds have on our imaginations and hearts, as you take in photos, paintings and prints that play with your entire concept of our wildlife and countryside. It's about watching and hearing some of the biggest names in birding showing off their knowledge and/or making fools of themselves at one of the many quizzes and panel shows upon the main stage.

It's being persuaded to part with your money and personal details by a bewildering array of businesses, NGOs, charities and other organisations (and, yes, *Bird Watching* magazine is among them). It does take willpower not to find yourself penniless after the first hour, but you'll return home with at least one classic field guide you thought you'd never find, or one shiny new pair of binoculars that will change your birding life. It's the powerful, phenolic flavour of whisky from Islay, and the sharp, refreshing kick of pisco sours from Peru, and it's steel bands from Trinidad and folk singers from the heart of England.

It's hearing the keynote lecture (speakers have included the likes of Sir David Attenborough) and knowing the message that's inspiring you will soon be winging its way around the world like a migrating bird.

Above all, it's about people. People you don't see from one year to the next, but who at some time or another have played a vital role in sparking and nurturing your own love of birds. People you've met on remote Scottish islands, or halfway up Andean volcanoes, or in the African bush. People who can change your life for the better, whether it's by persuading you to volunteer for a cause, or to travel to the destination you always wanted to see, and people who just want to share a beer or a coffee around the campfire and chat about the one thing all 25,000-plus attendees have in common – birds.

'There are thrills unspeakable in Rutland, more perhaps than on the road to Khiva.' So wrote a gentleman called Stephen Graham in 1923, in a book called *The Gentle Art of Tramping*. Whether you consider that Birdfair justifies his assessment probably depends on just how obsessed you are with birds; and the subtle, understated nature of Rutland's natural glories and picturesque towns can also tend to make it look like slight hyperbole.

But in recent years, Rutland has acquired one attraction that fully fits the billing, and I've left the crowds of the fair behind to find it. I head south from the main visitor centre, steadfastly ignoring the signs to a succession of hides named after some of the many species that visit Rutland Water or make it their home – tree sparrow, snipe, shelduck, and so on. I walk on past Lax Hill, and finally come out at wigeon hide, from where in winter you can watch big flocks of the eponymous ducks whistling as they feed.

The first of these birds could arrive any time now, but the stretch of the reservoir I'm looking at, Manton Bay, is known in summer for something else entirely. The hide, even with the competing draw of Birdfair, is almost full, and before I've had a chance to ask any of the occupants about our target, it shows up.

It's unmistakable. Short-tailed but long-winged, the latter distinctive by virtue of their four 'fingers' and the way they're held flexed at the carpal joint as the bird glides in from the left. It's pale, too – unusual among British raptors – and as we lift our binoculars and focus in, we can see the slight crest and the bandit stripe through the eye.

And then it stops. Unlike the kestrel, which stands absolutely motionless on the breeze as it hunts, the osprey's hovering is a little clumsy and heavy-winged, always on the verge of tipping over into forward flight or surrendering to the force of gravity.

But it's every bit as effective. Our bird has spotted a rich vein of silver just below the surface, and moves fast to stake its claim. Wings fold, and the bird drops, hitting the water with a loud splash. It's gone from sight for what feels like an age but can't be more than a couple of seconds, the bird transformed instantly into some strange creature of the deep, and then its head emerges from the lake, and its powerful wings haul it clear, back into the deep blue element that has been associated with birds from the earliest days. Even without optics, we can all see the trout it's carrying, slung in both talons, nose first, like a torpedo.

Ospreys are literally in a class of their own, one of the few bird species in the world to be in its own family. Found in most parts of the planet, they've adapted to catching fish, and absolutely nothing else. The fact they are found worldwide made their appearance in Rutland controversial, at least initially. Having become extinct in Britain between 1916 and 1954, with egg and skin collectors mainly to blame for their demise, they recolonised Scotland naturally: Scandinavian birds pass through Britain on their migration, so there was always a chance that some would stay to breed.

This recolonisation was slow but steady, and the species is under no threat globally, so a plan to release birds into the East Midlands with the intention of establishing a breeding population met with some opposition. Not just from fishermen, worried about what the raptors might catch, but from some birders who felt the money spent on the project would have been better used to meet other conservation priorities.

But the scheme went ahead, and it's hard to argue it hasn't worked. In 2014, for example, there were six pairs raising young at the reservoir and eighteen birds in total around the place; non-breeding youngsters often hang around likely nesting sites, checking out the possibilities for years to come.

Importantly, the Rutland ospreys have started to spread. Successful breeding pairs in Wales are birds that originally came from Rutland Water, and in the next few years this colonisation is likely to continue. The scheme's success is in encouraging other reservoirs to try to get in on the action. While a translocation scheme takes a lot of time, money and effort to implement, attracting a passing osprey or two to settle and breed is a far more feasible option; and so nesting platforms are starting to spring up across the Midlands and beyond, at places such as Carsington Water in Derbyshire.

Rutland's ospreys have had two more beneficial effects. They've captured the public's imagination as surely as an osprey snags one of the reservoir's tench, for starters. Special 'osprey cruises' on the lake are booked up months in advance; and if you visit Rutland Water's nature reserves any day between the middle of March and the middle of September, you can be sure every other birder you meet will ask if you've seen an osprey yet. On a local level, everyone from schoolchildren to local businessmen have got behind the birds, and it wouldn't be stretching things too far to say that the bird has helped bolster England's smallest county's sense of identity.

On an international level the project has built links between this country and Senegal and Gambia, the ospreys' main wintering grounds, and has created a far greater understanding of precisely what challenges these amazing birds face at all stages of their life cycle. There's that zooming-out feeling again: as I watch our osprey circling in front of the hide I'm transported to a sweltering African estuary, the high Atlas Mountains, parched Spanish steppes, a stormy Atlantic coastline, and everything in between.

Success has bred success, too. The popularity of the scheme, and its ability to pull in paying punters, has made Anglian Water more willing to put money into less glamorous, but equally vital, projects. Such as schemes to help tree sparrows, and water voles, and to extend and develop the lagoons so that Rutland Water will continue to be a site of the utmost importance to British wildfowl and waders in particular. This alone should justify the decision to reintroduce a species that isn't threatened on a global scale: every headline the ospreys grab is a step forward for the cause of conservation as a whole.

Over the next hour or so, the osprey perches on the dead limb of one of the trees just across the bay, alternating between pecking vigorously at the fish it caught, and gazing imperiously about. Birders come and go, and several of us attempt to read the ring on its leg identifying it, without success. Do so with a bird in the normal course of things and you can send the details of your sighting off to contribute to the great wealth of citizen science data that has added so much to the knowledge of British ornithologists. Do so with the ospreys, and you can go online and read about that particular bird's life story – the nest in which it was born, its journeys to Africa and back, breeding successes and failures, and so on. Technology such as satellite tracking devices combined with the dedicated work of volunteers from the Osprey Project, who travel to Africa each winter, and the generally high profile enjoyed by the scheme, mean we probably know as much about these individual wild birds as any others in history.

The hide has cleared by now, and there's a slight chill in the air to announce autumn's imminent arrival. The osprey is nowhere to be seen, either, having flapped leisurely away behind a screen of trees. I pack up slowly and walk back towards the visitor centre and Birdfair, wondering how long it will be before the raptor starts the long journey south.

They're not always in a hurry to get going, and even in those days when the nearest breeding birds were in Scotland, there was always a chance that a birder in another part of Britain would see an osprey during their spring and autumn migrations, as both the Scottish birds and those passing through from Scandinavia stop off to rest and fish whenever necessary. They don't need to eat from a larder the size of Rutland Water either – even very small bodies of water can attract their attention.

A few years ago, when most of my weekends were taken up with that most English of pastimes, village cricket, I was sitting with a teammate outside our pavilion. Our ground, flanked on one side by the town of Coalville (and specifically the factory that once made Action Man and Star Wars action figures), and on the other by the spoil heap of the old Snibston Colliery, generally attracted nothing more remarkable than a lot of pied wagtails and woodpigeons, but on this occasion we could see a couple of green woodpeckers snaffling ants in the short grass. I went to fetch some binoculars from the car to get a closer look, and a long-winged, pale shape soared out of the colliery compound and headed towards us. We both watched, open-mouthed, as an osprey flew no more than thirty feet above us, glancing down just once to take in the little cluster of white-clad figures, before finally settling on the trees around a little fishing lake at the back of the ground. In truth the pool looked barely more than a puddle to us, but it kept the raptor happy and well fed for a couple of days, before it continued on its odyssey.

The sighting marked another of those happy accidents, those chance encounters that make birdwatching so endlessly interesting and, yes, thrilling. You can make such occurrences more likely, and ensure you'll recognise them for what they are, by simply putting in the hours in the field, identifying and re-identifying the same, familiar species, on some occasions seeing next to nothing; but in the end such sightings still depend on luck, a certain breath of good fortune in the wind. Even if it's nothing as obviously remarkable as a fishing osprey, the chances are you will encounter something memorable – the way chaffinches turn into flycatchers to make the most of clouds of gnats, for example, darting out from treetop perches to launch themselves into the insect buffet, or the endlessly innovative riffing of a song thrush in full voice.

Birdfair, it suddenly occurs to me, works in the same way. You can do all your research beforehand and go there with a list as long as your arm, of products to try and destinations to talk about, and holidays to book, and causes to sign up to, and people to see and speak to – but you'll always come away carrying something you didn't expect, nestling in your rucksack or just turning over gently at the back of your mind.

I go through my own haul from the day. Details of how to stay on Britain's bird observatories, those coastal waystations that monitor the relentless push and pull of the tides of migration. An invitation to attend the United States' first-ever national bird fair. A second-hand copy of Simpson and Day's *Field Guide to the Birds of Australia* (for £4, how could I resist?). And a conversation with an old birder from my own neck of the woods, whose memories of breeding curlews fifty years ago throw new light on my own recent observations. These experiences help make light work of the dusty, footsore walk back into Oakham, and the heavy-lidded drowse homewards on the train, where the morning's babel of languages repeats itself, more quietly but with the good humour, if anything, deepened.

And then, as we near Leicester, travelling down the floodplain of the Wreake, there's a murmur of excitement, and necks are craned in the direction of a large flying silhouette that experience suggests might be a heron but hope turns into another osprey.

It is! There are enough binoculars to hand to make identification possible, even in the failing light, and you can feel the question emanating from every birdwatching mind in the carriage: is this some traveller from the far north, or one of the Rutland birds, its long journey triggered by a change in the light too subtle for our own eyes to notice?

We sit and watch as our own quietly contented worlds intersect one last time, as the osprey trails us at its own pace, following the train south into night, into the next day and who knows what awaits it.

9  Skyfall

'There! Right in front of us!'

The man to my right is talking in that tone of voice peculiar to birdwatchers, in which you try to communicate urgency and excitement without become so loud or so shrill that you frighten off the birds themselves. In this case, he's also having to deal with a particularly slow-on-the-uptake birder. Namely, me.

Suddenly, I see exactly what he means. A small, cryptically patterned bird is on the closely cropped ground just in front of a tussock of grass. The instant that it comes into focus in my binoculars I can see that it's a wryneck, a type of woodpecker now extinct in Britain as a breeding species, but which still pops up regularly on migration.

There's silence as we take in what we're seeing. I've seen these birds before in the UK, fleetingly, and I've had half-decent views in Hungary, but I've never seen one this clearly, or for so long. It resolutely refuses to do its neck-twisting threat display, where it transforms from bird into reptile before your very eyes, but that's no matter. It's clearly relaxed and feeding well on the ants around its feet, and so everybody's happy.

Being something of an outsider to the whole process of finding and identifying rare birds, I fail to defend myself to the exasperated man next to me, so I'll do it here. Put simply, the wryneck is a lot smaller than I'd expected, even having seen one before. You're thinking of a woodpecker, but you get something barely bigger than a bullfinch. Rather like famous people, birds are almost invariably smaller in real life than they appear in books or on TV.

Of course field guides always provide measurements to compare species, and some try to show the relative sizes of species on the same page. But despite their best efforts, nearly every birder sets out into the field with unrealistic expectations. I have a friend who says, only half-jokingly, that avocets never fail to disappoint him, because his books have led him to expect something the size of a crane. He's got a point: because waders tend to have long legs in proportion to their body size, you're geared to see something much larger than they actually are.

There's also the question of what we're used to. For many of us, or at least those not living close to wader hotspots, the one member of the family we grow up seeing regularly is the lapwing, despite recent declines. We then start to think of that as the default wader, and judge the size of all others by it. But the lapwing is actually a fairly large wader; the much more diminutive dunlin might be a much better yardstick to use. The same applies with ducks. When we are children, mallards and ducks are pretty much synonymous for us, and so we grow up failing to notice that mallards are actually one of the largest members of the duck family in Britain.

The thing is, it's a weekend for this sort of realisation. Rarity-chasing, or twitching as it's better known, has a bad name in some parts of the birdwatching community, and sometimes perhaps deservedly so, but the quest to see rarer species also has a lot to teach every birder ...

Yorkshiremen are famously not shy of singing the praises of the Broad Acres, so it's strange they should be quite so reticent about one of its greatest glories.

Or perhaps not. Here I am, surrounded by largely treeless agricultural land on either side of an unremarkable road. There's a village, and a cafe, and then the fields fall away and I'm travelling down a long spit of sand stitched together with marram grass. I slow the car instinctively, both to take in the view, with birds wheeling away to either side, and because I get the distinct feeling I might simply slip into the waves at any moment.

It might seem as though this place – Spurn Point – would be of interest only to geography students, as a classic example of longshore drift, in which the waters of the North Sea wash material from further up the east coast and deposit it in the relatively sheltered waters at the entrance of the Humber estuary. But for birdwatchers, it's been the scene of some of Britain's most notable sightings, and perhaps more importantly the country's most memorable 'falls', the term given to large numbers of migrant birds being deposited on our shores by weather systems.

Its importance for birds comes about partly because of its position. All headlands, spits and islands tend to be good places to look for migrants, because birds arriving off the sea naturally head towards the nearest and most obvious bit of dry land, while those working their way along a coast look for the shortest crossings of any estuaries or stretches of open sea. In autumn, as birds from northern England and Scotland, Iceland, Greenland and the Arctic move south, and those from Scandinavia, the Baltic and further east work their way south and west, Spurn can become a bottleneck, catching and funnelling birds down its length, as it gropes towards where, as Philip Larkin put it, 'sky and Lincolnshire and water meet'.

But birding hotspots also tend to benefit from a sort of self-fulfilling prophecy. If they're well known for attracting rare birds, then they also attract birdwatchers, and the more pairs of eyes there are 'working' them on a daily basis, the better the chances of the rare and scarce birds that pass through being spotted and logged. Spurn certainly falls into that category, as does somewhere like Cley on the north Norfolk coast, where several of Britain's best birdwatchers live. The Isles of Scilly, off Cornwall, once shared a similar reputation and attracted large numbers of birders each autumn, but visitor numbers have dropped in recent years because of a perception that the best transatlantic vagrants are being found further north, in the Western Isles or on Orkney and Shetland. That may be true, but it might also be down to more birders searching the latter, and less searching Scilly. It's a virtuous/vicious circle effect, and it's hard to extract the true nature of just how bird-rich any site is from it.

Similarly, some fantastic birdwatching spots, particularly those that are perceived as being aimed at the beginner or casual birdwatcher, probably don't get monitored as closely as they might: both Rutland Water and the RSPB's family-friendly but never disappointing reserve at Titchwell in Norfolk fall into this category. The tendency to overlook these sites might sometimes be the result of a sort of snobbishness among the more expert birders, but it's more likely due to the perception that such places are already well covered, when in fact they're not. In other words, everyone assumes that all the best birds each day will have been found by someone else, and promptly heads off to find their own somewhere else.

Spurn's popularity, however, endures, defying fad and fashion and the awesome power of the North Sea. A storm surge on 5 December 2013 was just the most recent example of the latter; in the later medieval period the sea claimed victory over two thriving towns along the peninsula. Ravenspurn was where Henry Bolingbroke (later Henry IV) landed in 1399 on his way to depose Richard II, while Edward IV arrived there in 1471 after going into temporary exile in the Netherlands. In times of old, nearby Ravenser Odd was a more important port than Kingston-upon-Hull, further along the estuary, but today both live on only as names in books, while Hull is a major city.

The December 2013 surge turned the Point into an island temporarily (in fact, it becomes one for a couple of hours on every particularly big tide) and washed away a road that was itself a temporary replacement for the previously eroded track. Fortunately for birders, Yorkshire Wildlife Trust, the owners of the site, have received support in restoring and maintaining it from both the RNLI, who built many of the buildings on the Point, and Spurn Bird Observatory, who monitor the birds passing through. And, importantly, Associated British Ports maintain a communications tower there for piloting ships in and out of the Humber estuary; all of which means that permanent loss of the road isn't an option, and there are plans to create a purpose-built visitor centre.

Nothing at Spurn, then, sits still. Not the organisations that own and run and maintain it; not the North Sea, remaking the maps and charts twice a day; and not the indomitable vegetation, working to make permanent what would otherwise be very temporary. The whole peninsula would, without man's intervention, move steadily westwards, and even with our help it's barely holding its ground.

And yet, the second lesson I learn here today, or relearn, I should say, is that sitting still is perhaps *the* most vital part of birdwatching. That seems odd. Twitching and rarity-watching are, after all, about dashing round the country in pursuit of birds, aren't they? Well, yes, sometimes, but if you're at a location like Spurn, where the birds are funnelled down a narrow strip of land, or anywhere else where there's a high concentration of birds, then the less you move the better.

Today I find a slightly sheltered spot on the south-eastern tip of the Point, among the marram grass, with the intention of photographing whatever comes my way. I'm no photographer, truth be told, but I get a lot of enjoyment out of taking 'record shots', pictures that are never going to win any awards for artistic achievement but which trigger fond memories of notable sightings during nostalgic winter evenings.

So I lie there on my side, with a view of the sea and the estuary's mouth and the flat, low expanse of Lincolnshire beyond. Even without the birds it would be a great place to watch the world go by, but once I remember to look behind me, too, at the low, wind-blown thicket of sea buckthorn, the birds start to arrive.

Whinchats. Lively birds the size of a robin, with broad eye stripes and a rusty, rufous stain to the breast. I see them only rarely at home, and declines have made them scarce in most parts of the UK, but for fifteen minutes there seems to be one on every bush, post and fence. I snap away with the camera, and scribble as many notes as I can, and then I look up, and they're gone.

They're soon replaced by a couple of male redstarts, and then a steady stream of warblers – willow, garden, blackcap and whitethroat, and another that only days later, after poring over my bad photos, do I identify as an icterine warbler, a regular but still noteworthy passage migrant here. There are three pied flycatchers, their smart black and white plumage of the spring browned and dulled by their busy summer. I'm too undisciplined in my observations to actually note where they're going: do they quickly gain height before making the jump across the Humber, then make their way further down the east coast, or do they work their way west and make the crossing where the river is narrower? Every time I decide to follow one little group, something else comes along to grab my attention. Another wryneck, and then a juvenile red-backed shrike. These 'butcher birds' – so-called because of their habit of impaling prey on thorns, to be eaten later – became extinct as breeders in the UK a few years back, but might just be creeping back in and raising young in a few scattered, and highly secret, southern locations.

This isn't the sort of day that's going to go down in Spurn folklore, when twitchers are drawn in as to a magnet, and yet it's quietly remarkable for any birder who, like myself, does most of their watching in a relatively small and ordinary inland patch. There are the numbers, for a start. I've already mentioned the whinchats, more in five minutes than I'd seen in five years, and the pied flycatchers, which continue to trickle through in twos and threes all day. But what's really incredible is how close they come. It's a photographer's dream. Even a bad photographer's dream.

In part, the birds might be so fearless because many of them arrive tired and in need of food and rest, and so they have little choice but to ignore the presence of humans. A lot of it, though, I realise, is down to me sitting there, not moving. An upright human signals danger to most birds (there's a reason why farmers used scarecrows), but reduce your profile and stay still, and they soon see you as far less of a threat. It's something I've noticed before when birdwatching from all sorts of boats, and oddly you often get the same effect from a vehicle, as long as you're driving slowly. Other birders assure me that riding a horse is better than either – the presence of a large herbivore clearly reassures birds considerably. But, for whatever reason, I'd forgotten until today just how effective keeping a low profile can be, and the rediscovery is every bit as much of a delight as seeing the likes of the shrike.

In fact, having relearned this lesson, I put it into practice near home a few days later. Not only do green woodpeckers and long-tailed tits settle in a tree just a couple of feet over my head, but a fox emerges from nearby scrub, shows mild surprise at my presence, then pads past unconcerned, like someone's dog out for a walk in the park.

There's another reason for the confiding nature of these migrants too, I suspect. Many are young birds, hatched earlier this year, and so many of them haven't had a chance to develop the wariness of humans on which their survival might, unfortunately, ultimately depend. Each time a little group of these juveniles passes through, I feel a sudden anxiety, a desire to keep them safe from the dangers that will assail them as they head into the distant south, assuaged a little by the thought that here, at least, they're among friends – as long as you don't count the sparrowhawk that periodically soars over the road, or the peregrine someone pointed out over the mudflats earlier.

I've already said I don't really consider myself a twitcher. For one thing, the long hours on the road don't appeal, nor does the thought of chasing all over the country in pursuit of birds that might not be there when you arrive. As I look around on this early autumn day, I realise this makes me something of a minority. Most of the birders here seem to be keen listers, and whenever I pass a little group, all the talk seems to be of the latest rarity they've seen, or very often the next one they're going to see.

It's this last aspect of twitching that sometimes troubles me. I can understand the feeling of delight and novelty at seeing a bird you've never seen in Britain before, even when it's a species that you've spotted easily elsewhere in the world. However many hoopoes you've seen while on holiday in Majorca, for instance, there's a delicious thrill when you're scanning a bit of coastal grassland and see a flash of orange, black and white resolve into this glorious bird, fanning its elaborate headdress as it lands. Seeing such a bird on the mundane surroundings of your own local patch, or even in a more unfamiliar but still distinctively British location, feels rather like spotting a Hollywood megastar in your local pub. Your own everyday world, narrow and flat and muted in colour as it can be, is suddenly touched with the glamour of something exotic. Even more importantly, you're reminded that everything doesn't proceed in a strictly textbook fashion. Anything can happen, and you have the proof in front of you.

Often the sighting of a rare bird is put to good use. If it's in a private location (and of course, plenty of rarities turn up in gardens and car parks and the like), a small charge can be made for access, with conservation charities benefiting. On one famous occasion, when a white-crowned sparrow (an American vagrant) turned up in Cley, Britain's most birdwatched parish, more than £6,000 was raised towards the local church's restoration fund, with the bird itself being immortalised in a new stained-glass window. Students of history might reflect on how appropriate it is that any sort of sparrow should benefit the church in this way: in the Venerable Bede's *Ecclesiastical History*, King Edwin of Northumbria is famously converted to

Christianity when a counsellor compares the life of pagan man to that of a sparrow which flits through the king's feasting hall in winter – a brief period of light and warmth, with cold, dark nothingness at either end.

But back to the present. What I can't get my head around is the speed with which some seasoned twitchers will put one sighting behind them and move on to the next. It can seem as though they're taking in little of what they see, and that the birds are no more than ticks on a checklist. The process looks uncomfortably like wishing your life away: that bird was great, but the next will be better ... At such times it's easy to see the addictive nature of twitching.

But I'm being very unfair. Most twitchers, for a start, are able to indulge in their chosen pastime purely because they're such good and experienced birdwatchers in the first place. Their trained eyes notice the smallest details of plumage, feather wear and structure and voice that casuals like myself would miss, so while twitchers might seem to be trailing around after other people's discoveries, they're generally far more likely than most of us to find rare birds in the first place.

And then there are the different levels of twitching. Most birdwatchers end up keeping some sort of list. You can't help but notice what you have and haven't seen in your garden, and the satisfaction you get the day a wintering blackcap shows up on your feeders is every bit as great as photographing a red-flanked bluetail on the east coast. Once you're a bit keener, you might start to keep a patch list, anything from the birds that you can see on foot from your front door, or at your nearest nature reserve, to the area covered by your local bird club. And you can subdivide these: a life list, for all-time sightings, and a year list, allowing you to compare trends over a long period of time. From there, you might move on to keeping a county list, something I've long done myself.

On the one hand, making lists makes perfect sense: bird records are still collected by county recorders, and many bird clubs and ornithological societies are organised on a county basis. On the other hand, listing can result in some slightly absurd situations. My own home in Leicestershire is less than ten miles from the borders of Derbyshire, Nottinghamshire, Staffordshire and Warwickshire, but the wish to add to my county list might send me off forty miles, to the far side of Oakham (Rutland still counts as Leicestershire, in my book) in search of species that appear regularly much closer to home, but on the wrong side of a boundary established over a thousand years ago. I witnessed the most extreme example of this a few years ago, when a juvenile squacco heron turned up at Attenborough Nature Reserve, just outside Nottingham, in late autumn. This attractive creature is a regular but scarce vagrant to Britain, so twitchers both national and local were out in force. But, as it was doing its fishing in a little stream flowing into one of the lakes, you could hear many of the local birders urging it to cross from one side to another, allowing them to tick it on both their Nottinghamshire and Derbyshire lists.

So perhaps there's not so much difference, after all, between the different tribes of birder. We all, I suspect, do our own form of twitching – and if for some it involves driving the length of the A1 to see a vagrant American wader, rather than pedalling frantically across town at lunchtime to see your first local rough-legged buzzard, who are we to judge?

Twitching, or any sort of birdwatching where rare birds are concerned, is all about context. Sit at Spurn on a day like today, and before long a single thought keeps recurring. Where are all these birds coming from?

The answers can be many and varied. Some of the birds are British breeders, and a migration-watch like this can make you realise that just because something is rare or scarce on your own patch, it isn't everywhere else. But most must be coming from further afield, from a great arc of the planet curving from Iceland and Greenland, through Scandinavia, and on into central and eastern Europe, and the forests of Siberia beyond that.

Once you get your head around this, the often astonishing numbers of birds make sense. Falls like those which have deposited hundreds and thousands of redstarts, say, on the east coast, can seem absolutely incredible to us in the UK, where such a bird is nowhere particularly numerous. But travel to the forests of Eurasia, and hear redstart after redstart singing day after day, and you realise that such a fall is but a drop in the ocean. North-easterly and easterly winds might push big groups our way, but there'll be even more days when even larger groups disappear south without ever coming near Britain.

I was in Latvia recently, and whinchats and wood warblers were everywhere. At home, these birds would warrant a mention on my local bird group's website, and they'd probably spark a minor local twitch, with all the seasoned Leicestershire listers turning up to get them on their county list for the year. But our Latvian guides barely noticed them, unsurprisingly, so used are they to their presence. The same went for bitterns: their booming was the constant soundtrack to most of the trip, yet they meant far more to us Brits than they did the locals, starved as we are of these gloriously strange birds.

We stood at one site, listening to a bittern's low-frequency courtship call, sometimes compared to blowing across the open neck of a bottle, but actually rather like a mobile phone vibrating on a wooden table; believe me, I tried to answer the bittern half-a-dozen times before I twigged. As we watched, a familiar sight drifted across the pool in front of us without any of us registering it, until our guide delightedly pointed out that this was his first Canada goose of the year, the species being a major rarity in Latvia rather than the ubiquitous toddler-botherer it is here.

And so twitching is really about noticing what's different, what's new, what's out of place. At its best it's a way of honing skills and testing them against the bewildering variety of birds that can be thrown your way (the best twitchers don't necessarily accept an initial ID until they've seen it with their own eyes). It can help highlight conservation priorities, and raise funds to address them. It can increase our knowledge of migration routes and timings.

Above all, it's about remembering that this is a world in constant motion, in which a whole continent's birds can move en masse to another, with a diversion or two along the way. And nowhere is better to see and understand this fact than at Spurn, where the land itself is as provisional as the winds, and the frailty of its finger, pointing the way south, mirrors the precarious existence of the birds that pass through.

10 Of a Single Mind

British poets like birds. Or at least, they like to write about birds. From anonymous Anglo-Saxon bards listing the seabirds of the wild and windy northern firths, through Chaucer's *Parliament of Fowls*, to the nineteenth-century Romantics and their nightingales and skylarks, birds have been co-opted as metaphors and symbols ever since the English language was first written down. In modern times, this tendency shows no signs of abating. Just a decade or so ago, a flick through the pages of small-press poetry magazines would have revealed a preoccupation with seagulls. And, yes, 'seagulls' was the word used. You can imagine the paroxysms of anger experienced by any birders who read it.

These days, starlings have taken the seabirds' place. Starlings strutting round gardens and lording it over the other birds at the feeders. Starlings singing their strange, half-improvised, half-stolen songs from atop TV aerials (although not for much longer, presumably). And starlings swirling and swooping in cloud-like flocks that even non-birders can tell you, without a moment's hesitation, are called murmurations.

Admittedly I'm speaking with something of a vested interest, but I think the poets might have it right in this instance. Starlings might just be the most poetically resonant of all British birds. Not because they're the most beautiful, or the most astounding in their behaviour – although they're both – but because, more than with any other species, we each of us see them in our own way, and make of them what we will.

A murmuration is a prime example of that. It's the end of October, and I'm standing on a slightly muddy path half an hour or so before dusk, back on the Somerset Levels where this whole business began. Scope and tripod are set up and waiting by my side, my binoculars are round my neck, and half-a-dozen similarly attired and equipped birdwatchers are strung out along maybe two hundred yards of path, some chatting with each other. There's an elderly couple, too, armed with compact binoculars barely bigger than opera glasses, who tell me they've dropped in on the way back to their holiday cottage. They're not birdwatchers – they want to be very clear about that – but they've heard what to expect here and they're not about to miss it. Further along the path there's another little knot of four men, all hefting Canon or Nikon DSLRs with huge zoom lenses. They talk among themselves, an arcane language of f-stops and ISO and auto-focus.

The conditions are perfect. A clear sky and little wind mean that when the first birds start to coagulate into a group, and then a full-blown flock, we can see it happen a mile off, quite literally. There are maybe twenty birds to start with, skimming low over the reeds and twisting and turning back and forth, but more appear, and quickly the twenty becomes two hundred. I don't notice where the newcomers have come in from – I'm too busy focusing on the movements of the original nucleus – but some of them may well have flown thirty miles to reach this point.

By the time the murmuration has gathered four thousand or so participants, the cameras are clicking away merrily, and we watchers on the path are doing plenty of murmuring ourselves. We all seem compelled to call out loud the shapes the flock takes as the birds manoeuvre over the marsh: a flying saucer, a whale, a double-helix! Even, for one brief moment, a huge bird that spreads its wings then folds into a tight, black ball against the oranges and pinks of the sunset. For the photographers, this is what it's all about – capturing the moment at which thousands of essentially everyday birds become something else entirely.

And the flock carries on getting bigger and bigger, as if every starling in Somerset was an iron filing hopelessly attracted to a giant magnet. When one of its swoops brings it lower and closer, we can hear the rush of massed wings, and a certain amount of chatter, and the impression that we're seeing and hearing a single living entity is stronger than ever. It puts me in mind of one of the dragons of Nordic legend passing over.

That just reflects my own preoccupations, though. One of the photographers talks of galaxies of birds, spinning and spiralling away into blue space, and it's hard to disagree. Another describes them as a firework display in negative. And the elderly couple, the defiantly non-birding pair, well, they might just hit the nail on the head: the movement resembles one of those speeded-up films of flowers blooming and withering, blooming and withering, they tell me. I nod.

The birds are what we want them to be, and they make poets of all of us.

Murmurations have made starlings a favourite of another select group of people – the newspaper subeditors and designers of Britain. Having worked as one of the former for many years myself, I can vouch for the utterly dispiriting feeling that descends on the newsroom some time after lunch on a slow day in winter, when there are still gaping great holes on a couple of the inside pages, and little prospect of anything happening to fill them.

Which is where starlings fly to the rescue. Their pre-roost gatherings – for that is what a murmuration is – have for years drawn the attention of any number of amateur photographers, as well as the press's staff snappers. Keep a few of them on file, and you've got an eye-catching, beautiful space-filler for page 13.

All of which means that starlings enjoy a higher profile in the public consciousness than just about any other British bird species. Everyone, but everyone, knows that those dense but amorphous clouds of birds swirling across the page are starlings, and more than a few people will be inspired enough to go out looking for them in the flesh. Most people know that collective noun – murmuration. It's a good one, because it conjures up both the complex vocalisations of this rowdy bird, subdued a little by distance, and the noise made by the massed wings of the flock sweeping back and forth; and it certainly feels more poetic than another of the collective nouns used for this species: an 'affliction'. A third – a 'chattering' – is a perfectly straightforward and perfectly accurate description of a group of starlings on the ground, or perched; it's rare that they'll stay silent for long in such a situation.

So, while those hacks might have the (understandably) selfish motive of filling the paper as quickly as possible, over the last twenty years or so they've done the image of the

starling an awful lot of good. And it was certainly an image
that needed a boost.

Sometimes, when murmuration pictures appear in the press,
there's little more than an extended caption, telling you
where the photographer spent yesterday afternoon, watching
and waiting for the birds to gather. Sometimes, though, an
enterprising subeditor has decided that the image needs a bit
of context, and will dig around online for some recent research
into exactly why the birds do what they do. And there's no
shortage of theories (which makes for more copy to fill space),
but no definitive answer.

Which is to say, we know why starlings, and other birds such
as waders, gather into large roosting flocks at night. There's
safety in numbers, for a start: any predator has far more
chance of being seen or heard by thousands of eyes and ears.
There's warmth, too: the body heat of dozens of neighbours is
available to help any individual starling make it through the
cold night. And, although we don't really understand how it
works, there's information exchange: the birds manage to pass
on to each other exactly where the best feeding spots are for
the day ahead.

What we haven't worked out yet is exactly why starlings
perform such intricate, extended pre-roost aerobatics. If safety
is the paramount concern, does it really make sense to take to
the air and advertise your presence to every predator within
miles? If keeping warm is top of the agenda, isn't all that flying
around a waste of vital energy? And if information exchange is
what it's all about, surely that's better done in a more relaxed
fashion?

The likelihood is that all those motivations are outweighed by another consideration, which is the desire to create as large a flock as possible, and so maximise all of those other potential benefits. To do this, the original nucleus of the flock makes sure that it will be seen from as far away as possible. The more members that join, the more visible it becomes, and so the flock starts to feed on its own success.

Not every flock is successful, of course. The big murmurations – the ones that come to the attention of newspapers and TV programmes – usually centre on reed beds, or woodland, or sometimes man-made structures; but that doesn't mean there aren't smaller ones here, there and everywhere. Wherever they happen, the pre-roost aerobatics are part of the deal.

And that's what's unusual. Other birds that gather to roost generally do so more unobtrusively, or straightforwardly. Corvids and gulls head towards their overnight sites purposefully and directly, as do waders. My late afternoon journeys home from the office in autumn often start with straggling flocks of lapwings scudding low over the A1 before dropping straight into some flooded fields on the far side. And while waders such as knot and dunlin do perform mass flying displays to rival those of starlings, these also occur when they leave the roosts in the morning, or when moving between sites because of the advancing tide. No other species makes such a ritual of things as the starling.

If we don't know exactly why starlings do what they do, when they do, we are at least closer to knowing how they do it. Research in recent years, using computer modelling, has helped us to understand just how thousands of birds can fly together almost wing to wing, without constant collisions and resulting mayhem. It seems that, regardless of how far away they actually are from each other, each starling bases its directional decisions on its nearest neighbours; whereas it had been thought previously that starlings took note of the position of every bird within a certain distance. The new model makes more sense: it only requires each bird to remain aware of the movements of half-a-dozen or so others, while maintaining flexibility and cohesion.

Marvelling at murmurations isn't, as it turns out, a modern development at all. *The Exeter Book*, a tenth-century anthology that is the largest surviving collection of Anglo-Saxon literature, contains around ninety riddles. Some of them involve double entendres that would have failed to make the cut in a *Carry On* film, while others are relatively straightforward. One of them, in a recent translation by the poet Gary Soto, describes 'small creatures ... feathery as grain, fine as smoke ... angling for the green pond but not touching down.' Reading it, the average Briton, let alone the average British birder, will come up with the answer: starlings.

But, importantly, the unknown Anglo-Saxon poet was confident that his mead-hall audience would know the answer too. 'We folks know them from a distance,' he asserts in Soto's version, conjuring up a picture of both *thegn* and *ceorl* – which is to say 'nobleman' and 'peasant' – lifting their heads briefly from the day-to-day trials and tribulations of the Dark Ages to marvel at the kaleidoscopic wonder unfolding before them. Or perhaps they just wanted to eat them; the Anglo-Saxons, as we've seen before, tended to view birds primarily in terms of their nutritional value.

The gatherings have continued to inspire poets over the years. The Romantic poet Samuel Taylor Coleridge, a keen observer of the natural world like most of his ilk, was moved to write a description of a murmuration in the winter of 1799, saying:

> Starlings in vast flights drove along like smoke, mist, or any thing misty without volition – now a circular area inclined in an Arc – now a Globe – now from complete Orb into an Elipse & Oblong – now a balloon with the car suspended, now a concaved Semicircle – & still it expands & condenses, some moments glimmering & shivering, dim & shadowy, now thickening, deepening, blackening!

As well as celebratory there's something faintly ominous about the way Coleridge's description progresses, but as mentioned earlier perhaps one of the reasons we like starling murmurations so much is that we can make of them what we will.

Throughout the centuries, starlings remained widespread and incredibly numerous birds. After the Second World War, and with the country in the twin grip of Cold War tensions and Space Age speculation, unexplained contacts started to show up on the increasingly powerful radars being used. Known as 'angels', they were tagged as UFOs, potential flying saucers, until someone started to notice that their movements matched those of the huge flocks of starlings that roosted in London each night, and moved out towards more open country each morning.

No doubt the decline was already setting in, but when I started birdwatching starlings were still incredibly numerous. Flocks of thirty or so regularly turned up on our suburban back lawn, strutting around with the agitated air of someone being forced to walk through a crowded shopping centre while wearing a straitjacket. Aggressive and noisy, they dominated the feeders. At about that time, the councils of various British cities were considering all sorts of drastic action to minimise the damage caused by huge, incontinent roosts of the birds all over their historic buildings. When I went to university in Newcastle-upon-Tyne, for example, in 1988, you could watch the starlings gathering at dusk each day to settle on the ledges and sills of the Georgian streets sweeping down to the river.

Since then, they've suffered a steep and worrying decline of around 50 per cent since 1995, with a dearth of nesting sites (as the older buildings they favour get replaced or renovated), and lack of insect food later in the summer (badly hitting second and third broods) getting the blame. They've become one of those species that, depending on where in the country you live, can appear to be as common as they ever were, or completely extinct.

The truth is, there are still an estimated 800,000 breeding territories in the UK, with numbers boosted further in winter by the arrival of millions of migrants from central and eastern Europe, and Scandinavia. Occasionally, the birds still cause the sort of consternation and alarm that novelist Daphne du Maurier would have appreciated. In parts of Britain, including East Anglia, farmers consider them an agricultural pest, and apply for licences to cull them; although how much good that does is a matter for great debate – you'd have to shoot an awful lot of starlings to make an appreciable difference, and even then you'd probably only create a feeding opportunity for more starlings, or other species.

But the general public aren't safe, either. In February 2014, residents of a Hereford street told the national newspapers about the snowstorm of droppings that descended upon them when a flock of starlings started roosting in a nearby leylandii hedge. That hedge is significant, because every birder you speak to will tell you that, however plentiful the species still is in some locations, it's less and less likely to be found in woodland. Back in the 1970s, when I started birding, the woods and forests were full of these birds, but while doing a monthly survey of a local deciduous wood over the last year, I haven't seen a single starling.

It's taken me a few years to appreciate it, but Heathrow Central Bus Station has its charms, despite the noise, fumes, crowds and delays. I'm sitting on one of the outside benches waiting for the 230 service, and it's raining and blowing an autumn gale. So far, so British, but I've just spent the past week in South Africa, travelling through the Kruger National Park and up the east coast in search of birds and some of the world's most iconic mammals under clear skies and blazing sun, so I'm feeling the opposite of homesick.

Among the highlights were violet-backed starlings, amethyst gems that glittered and flared under the unceasing Natal sun, and whose wheezing, buzzing, busy songs gave away their relationship to our own sole representative of this large Old World family (although the common starling has been introduced elsewhere, notably the United States, where it is considered a pest). And as I sit here, flicking through the new edition of *Birds of Southern Africa*, reliving a week's worth of 'lifers' (the birder's term for a bird they've seen for the first time ever), there's a wheezing and buzzing from somewhere close at hand, and then two starlings arrive on the forecourt and commence their usual self-important parading around in search of food.

There are more, too, because from a little further away they're answered with not only the same harsh, chattering racket, but also a collection of other sounds accrued in a lifetime of foraging in this most human of landscapes. A mobile phone's ringtone. The hum and swish of electric doors. The warning beeps of a reversing coach, of course. Listen to any starling for long enough, and you're taken on a trip through every location of its life. They're avian samplers, relentless collectors of their aural surroundings, recyclers of the hummadruz of modern urban life. That's because they are, in fact, closely related to mynahs, among the most renowned of avian mimics, which alone ought to be enough for them to throw off their dowdy image.

But look at them! Seriously – stop for a moment, and take a long, hard look at the next one that crosses your path, even if, like the one I'm watching, it's picking its way around the edge of a gutter with its bill crammed full of discarded sandwich and dropped crisps. OK, so they'll never win any awards for elegance: their flight silhouette is compact and functional, rather than rangy and dashing, and we've already talked about that ungainly, busy gait. But their colours and markings make up for all that.

When they are seen close up, in winter, it's hard to know where to start. The way their apparent coal blackness at a distance disintegrates into a glorious swirl of blues and greens and purples as the light catches them, like the rainbow film of petrol on the drizzly tarmac in front of me. Or that constellation of stars radiating out from just below the bill? If this were a species that only turned up here once in a blue moon, as a vagrant on the east coast, for example, we'd go running to see it and photograph it and sketch it without a second thought. As it is, even now when the starling is far less common than previously, we rarely give it a second glance.

And while, as we've seen, this bird is deeply ingrained in our culture, it's also strangely out of focus. That is, it's always been there, but rarely the centre of attention; or else it's co-opted as a metaphor, or forming part of a crowd scene. The reason, of course, is that it's always been so common and widespread.

Who needed to make a fuss about something that could be seen without effort?

So, as high as murmurations figure in our pantheon of natural wonders, isn't it time to give the starling a bit more individual attention? Every one of them is a masterpiece in miniature, an exotic in exile, a wonder in itself, and a muse for every one of us.

11 Dark Stars

It had to happen, sooner or later. Part of the appeal of birdwatching lies in the fact that nothing is guaranteed; and so, eventually, I was bound to draw a blank in my quest. I just hadn't expected this particular part of it to prove so difficult.

In 2007, a book called *Crow Country* hit the shelves. Written by Mark Cocker, who a couple of years earlier had been responsible for the magnificent *Birds Britannica*, it gave corvids the moment in the spotlight they so richly deserve. Here they were in all their glory. Among the most intelligent of birds, their rich and complicated social lives were opened up. Those who had previously dismissed them as 'trash' birds gazed on them with a newfound respect and fascination, while non-birders developed a more nuanced view of them than warranted by their previous roles as birds of ill-omen or coldly efficient cleaners of roadkill from our blood- and fur-spattered roads.

The book also recounts the author's fascination – some would say obsession – with one particular aspect of corvids: their propensity for forming huge, noisy roosts. Cocker describes how, at Buckenham Carrs, close to his Norfolk home, the skies were darkened each dusk by the passage of around 40,000 rooks and jackdaws heading back to the communal gathering. What emerges most strongly from the book is not only the staggering scale and grandeur of this phenomenon, but the complicated motivations the birds have for coming together in this way.

And so I wanted to see for myself what all the fuss was about, to get just a hint of the complex social life – every bit as complex as our own, in fact – that these birds possess.

I failed.

The first time I tried, not that long after *Crow Country* came out, I happened to be passing through the area and decided, on a whim, to give it a shot. Noël Coward famously dismissed Norfolk as 'very flat', but its undulations, unspectacular as they are, can't be ignored by the birdwatcher. The spot described by Cocker is in a wide, shallow river valley, but on this particular day, twenty feet in altitude made a world of difference. Back at the main road, or in the village close to the roost, it was a fine evening, with sun still bright through a slight haze. But down on the floodplain, a thick mist had descended, hiding anything that lay more than a few feet away. I stood, occasionally hearing the croak and bark of corvids passing overhead, but even those sounds were muffled by the cold, clammy blanket.

Actually, I shouldn't have been surprised. Family legend tells of a summer holiday, when I was three or four, in Sheringham in north Norfolk. My parents had booked a caravan for two weeks in August, but for the first seven days the whole of East Anglia was wrapped in a thick and all-enveloping fog. They abandoned any thoughts of the beaches, and instead tried to interest two small children in the county's other attractions; finally despairing, they headed home to Leicestershire. There they encountered their next-door neighbour, stripped to the waist and bronzed after a week of gardening in blazing sunshine. So, after a day or two's recovery, they looked at the forecast, and seeing that prospects for Norfolk seemed to be brighter, headed back east along the A47, thinking they might as well make use of the caravan they'd paid for. And it all looked good, until they reached Sheringham, and found it still cocooned in its immovable fog. I remember nothing of all this except a ride on a steam train (which at the time would have assuaged my disappointment considerably), but the story, retold every summer, gave me an unreasonable prejudice against the county of Nelson until my late twenties, when knowledge of its birding riches finally became too much to ignore.

I've failed again today – and once more the weather was to blame. It was raining when I got there, a thin but all-enveloping November mizzle, and it was raining when I left; and although the precipitation never became more than a steady drizzle, it was enough to dilute the longed-for clouds of corvids to a steady but thin overcast of rooks and jackdaws that finally fizzled out just before sunset – and which fell a long way short of anything truly memorable.

Then something strange happens. Over the next couple of weeks I'm shown that what happens at Buckenham Carrs is only one example of something that goes on right across the UK: a twice-daily movement of wildlife on a massive scale, were you to tot up the biomass involved.

I see the same thing from the M1, for example: a long, purposeful stream of rooks making their way from freshly ploughed fields near Loughborough to some colony I've never seen, yet which might have been in place since the Vikings arrived in these parts, or before. Then I'm surprised late one Sunday afternoon when, as we sit watching TV, across the one small patch of sky visible from my girlfriend's sofa, a loose, voluble straggle of jackdaws makes the commute from the sheep pastures to their roosting sites on the church and the older houses in the village. One evening not long afterwards,

the sky close to the office is suddenly filled with a dense, swirling storm of ragged black wings, lifted from the soil by who knows what alarm or signal.

And I start to grow a little obsessed myself. Corvids have always been among my favourite birds. I blame a teenage flirtation with gothdom – the original, 1980s incarnation, which involved listening to The Cure and Sisters of Mercy, not the more recent American phenomenon, with all its vampire nonsense. I find myself tracking the movements of particular groups of corvids as best I can. I leave the house ten minutes earlier each morning, so my route to work will intersect the passage nearby of a particular rook colony to the fields on the edge of the village. I notice the single-minded way they head straight to each day's designated feeding area, and how one sheep pasture can hold a couple of hundred of these smartly trousered creatures (carrion crows, on the other hand, have tight-fitting knickerbockers), while the apparently identical pasture next door has not one. As Mark Cocker found out, and described with such precision and beauty, corvids have a deep and complicated relationship with the people of these islands.

TV and film sound-effects people, even in this digital age in which practically any noise in the world should be only a few mouse clicks away, often paint their sound pictures using a surprisingly restricted palette. Need something to evoke a wild, lonely night in a northern wilderness? The eerie sound of the great northern diver (common loon, to Americans) is just the job, and failing that the mewing call of a red-tailed hawk. Never mind that the former is rare in the UK, and the latter unknown – both regularly pop up on British TV. You could, were you to go out into the street at such times, probably hear the low but steady rattle and chatter of a million birdwatchers shaking their heads.

Likewise, any scenes in woodland tend to take place to the backdrop of the spring songs of common species, regardless of the time of year or the area of Britain being portrayed. And, if you need a sort of auditory shorthand for traditional British farmland, then there's only one option – the insistent cawing of rooks. Actually, if the programme in question is set in autumn or winter, this sound isn't a bad choice at all. Go for a walk pretty much anywhere outside the highland regions of these islands between October and March, and the harsh, flat 'kaaa' of the rook is likely to be your accompaniment at some point, perhaps mixed with the lively 'chack' of the jackdaw, or the harsher but more vibrant 'kraa' of the carrion crow.

You might have noticed something about the names of all three of those species. They're imitative of the actual sound the bird makes (well, in the jackdaw's case, the first part of the name is). They're far from unique in this respect, of course – cuckoo is probably the best-known example among British birds – but no other bird family contains such a concentration of monikers like this. Three other members of the family – raven (from Old Norse *hrafn*), chough and jay – have similarly onomatopoeic names, leaving only the now-ubiquitous magpie and that ultra-rare vagrant, the nutcracker, as the odd ones out.

It would be perfectly reasonable to assume that there must be a reason for our fascination with these birds, and in fact there's very likely several. All our corvids are, for a start, birds of reasonable size. The raven is by far the biggest, with a size and bulk roughly equivalent to the buzzard, but even the jackdaw is a step up from most of our familiar garden birds, so we tend to notice them when they cross our path. Secondly, they tend to have very easily identified plumages – all black in most cases; black and white in the magpie's; or a positively gaudy combination of pink, black, white and blue in the jay's. So, corvids are visually conspicuous. Their calls also tend to be loud, frequent, resonant and distinctive, which means that even if we can't see them, we're rarely left in any doubt that they are in the vicinity.

But there is, I suspect, another reason (albeit one linked with the fact that you always know when a corvid's around). It's as well that crows are strong flyers, because they carry with them perhaps a greater weight of association and implication than any other British bird family. True, other birds such as wrens have a great deal of folklore and superstition attached to them, but none of them match the corvids for their ability to instantly create an impression, even among people who have no real interest in birds.

That impression is, admittedly, a bad one. Corvids are irrevocably associated with evil at worst, and a general sense of darkness and gloom at best. This probably has something to do with the fact that for centuries corvids (ravens especially, but no doubt many of the smaller species too) were known as carrion birds that appeared after battles to feast on human flesh. We have no vultures in Britain, so they would have been by far the most common participant in these gory banquets, and a glance through any general book on British history will remind you just how many battles there were in these islands until the middle of the eighteenth century. Traditional ballads such as 'The Three Ravens' and its variants (including the more cynical 'Twa Corbies') reflect that flesh-eating history.

Ravens were also seen as distinctly un-Christian, even actively pagan birds. Odin, the Norse god of battle, had two ravens, Huginn and Muninn, or 'Thought' and 'Memory', whom he sent out into the world each day, and who reported back to him each night on all they had seen and heard. When the Vikings started their raids, and then invasions of Britain from the late eighth century onwards, they generally did so beneath a distinctive banner bearing the device of a raven; and that alone would explain why the early medieval church, and the general populace, might have developed a negative view of the largest corvid.

Even before the Vikings, of course, the Christian church might have frowned upon the raven's use in iconography and decoration. Before their conversion, the Anglo-Saxons had had their own version of Odin – Woden – and it's reasonable to suppose that he too might have been accompanied by raven familiars. Ravens, then, were given a bad press for a whole host of reasons, and the rest of the corvid family might well have been damned by association. Add to that the fact they can – especially rooks and jackdaws – be seen as agricultural pests, and you have a recipe for disdain, and worse.

That disdain shows itself in the collective nouns used for corvids. Although some of these were coined relatively recently, in the nineteenth century, and are deliberately either whimsical or attention-grabbing, others go back much further, and corvids don't come out of it well. A group of crows is described as a rather menacing-sounding 'horde', an even more threatening 'mob', or a downright malevolent 'murder', while a gathering of ravens is an 'unkindness'.

Shakespeare reflects these attitudes in *Macbeth*, in which he touches upon one of the more curious facts about the British corvid family – and one that still ensures that some of these birds are blamed for crimes they didn't commit. As Macbeth reassures his wife about the planned murder of Banquo, he uses the crow's malevolent associations in a speech full of foreboding and doom:

... Light thickens, and the crow
Makes wing to th' rooky wood.
Good things of day begin to droop and drowse;
While night's black agents to their preys do rouse.

Macbeth seems to be in some doubt as to whether it's crows or rooks he's talking about (although it's perfectly possible that the former might nest very near the latter), and it's easy to see how rooks, and the jackdaws that are often found with them, might be tarred with the same carrion-eating, lamb-attacking brush as ravens and crows, merely because they look similar. However, the worst that rooks and jackdaws can fairly be accused of is damaging the occasional crop, and even this is hugely outweighed by the favour they do farmers by acting as natural pest-controllers: rooks, in particular, have a liking for leatherjackets and other larvae and grubs.

But matters were no doubt as unclear in Shakespeare's time, and in the fictionalised version of the eleventh century he was writing about in the Scottish play, as they are now. For instance, Scotland has two versions of the crow. South and east of the Great Glen, there are all-black carrion crows just like anywhere else in Britain. North and west of it, however, there are hooded crows – handsome grey and black birds that were once thought to be merely a subspecies of the former. And all along the 'borderline' between the two there are fertile hybrids.

As if that's not enough, in Scotland the rook can seem a quite different bird from the version we see in England and Wales. True, there are some enormous rookeries on rural estates in Aberdeenshire, bigger than anywhere else in the UK, but Scottish rooks also seem a lot more adventurous than their Sassenach counterparts; and that's when telling them apart from their cousins gets really difficult.

A few years ago, I travelled up to St Andrews in spring to read at StAnza, the large poetry festival there. I had three great days catching up with friends, meeting and listening to new writers, and enjoying the sort of warm welcome that Scotland does better than just about anywhere else on earth. I was also determined to make the most of the bright, blustery March weather by going birdwatching. And so I did. The fulmars were already back on the cliffs, mini-albatrosses returned after a winter's wandering. There were curlews on the beaches and the flooded fields and the golf courses, gracefully picking up choice morsels. There were gulls, of course. And there were rooks.

They were not in the trees, nor on the ploughed fields, but strutting up and down the main street, rooting around in litter bins, perched on guttering and ridge tiles, and generally behaving in every way like carrion crows (of which there were none). I gave in to my fondness for this particular avian family, and spent hours watching as they confidently exploited every feeding and roosting opportunity that the grand old town could offer them. Their adaptability and ingenuity shouldn't have come as any surprise, corvids being renowned for such things, but their willingness to live right next to man, and man's willingness to tolerate them in return, was unusual.

Elsewhere, the old attitudes linger on. All the corvids, even the jay, appear on the list of pest species that farmers can shoot or otherwise control, and despite the considerable consciousness-raising effect of Mark Cocker's book, there's still a distinct shortage of people willing to speak up for this much-misunderstood tribe. I'd like to try to reverse that, even if only a little.

Ahead of me, the peaks of Snowdonia are glinting in the last of the sun. Early snows, perhaps, lying in some of the higher corries and cwms, or maybe just surface water or the first hard frost.

For the last two days, I've been exploring some of the gentler trails. While they can provide pretty lean pickings for birders in autumn and winter, the 'gronk, gronk' of ravens has been a regular – in fact, a constant – accompaniment to my ramblings. Now I'm sitting, huddled, on the edge of Newborough Warren, wondering whether any of the birds I'm about to see are actually old acquaintances.

The Warren – it was colonised by rabbits in the Tudor period – sits on the southern point of Anglesey, the largely flat, fertile island that was once the granary of the Welsh princes through the centuries. It's a large expanse of dunes, some fixed, others constantly on the move as if reaching out towards the mainland, tantalisingly close across the Menai Strait. Areas have become forested, and there's a lake, a saltmarsh and mudflats.

This is the home of Britain's most renowned raven roost. I'm keen to see whether or not its glittering reputation is entirely deserved, in the light of some of the tales I've been told. Some claims put the number of birds gathering here at around 2,000, or at least they say that was the figure when the roost was at its peak five or six years ago, adding that birds come from as far afield as Ireland, the Isle of Man, north-west England, and even southern Scotland. That would be a very significant chunk of the British population: there's reckoned to be around 8,000 breeding pairs in total across these isles.

Other watchers feel those figures are too high, and that the same birds may have been counted more than once; whatever the case, the numbers are now somewhat down. What isn't up for dispute is that even now, in its diminished state, it's one of the largest such roosts in the world, still attracting 800 to 1,000 birds, and there are satellite roosts elsewhere on Anglesey, at Mynydd Bodafon and Pentraeth.

As I watch, they start to arrive from the east. A pair, although most of the roost's members will probably be unpaired younger birds. Field guides often include useful tips on how to identify ravens, such as noting the diamond shape of the tail as they fly, the huge, heavy, chisel-like bill, the shaggy throat feathers, and the long wings – and pointers like these can all be useful, given that the bird's size isn't always obvious without any context.

Nothing, however, is quite so distinctive as the tendency for ravens to indulge in all sorts of stunning aerobatics, tumbling, rolling and even flying upside-down, often seemingly just because they can. I've seen this characteristic in the ravens nesting just outside my home village. I've seen it in ravens high in the Scottish mountains. And I've seen it, memorably, in Extremadura, in Spain, when a group of four winging their way high over the open plains took turns to show off, as though to alleviate the monotony of the miles of flatland they faced before they reached the distant mountains.

This pair do exactly that, now, suddenly folding like clenched, black-gloved hands, then plummeting groundwards, before righting themselves and carrying on as though nothing had happened. When more arrive, in loose groups of twos and threes and more, most do the same, or add their own variations, including barrel rolls. It's as if they can't bear not to use the skills they have at their disposal.

And so it continues. I try to keep count as best I can, but the birds are arriving not only from the mainland, but also from behind me and away to the left. Ravens, after all, when left to themselves are extremely catholic in their tastes where habitat is concerned, so much so that Max Nicholson, in *Birds of the Western Palearctic*, commented: 'so wide-ranging that concept of habitat is hardly applicable'. Today's birds, I guess, have been everywhere from the tops of the mountains to the seashore itself, taking in everything in-between, including man-made landscapes such as landfill sites. It's only because the bird was persecuted and hounded away from the haunts of man for so much of the last two centuries that we've come to think of it as a creature of the mountains, cliffs and other upland places.

Their foraging will have turned up an eclectic menu to match: worms, hikers' dropped sandwiches, dead fish and seals, human rubbish, roadkill and just about anything else you can think of, including a range of other carrion. In Wales, hill sheep will be among that latter category, including, in spring, their dead lambs, although ravens have long been blamed for killing live lambs, too. When I was a child, I remember more than one elderly relative telling me that ravens habitually pecked the eyes out of lambs, and so they were the bogeyman of my early birding world – beings more fierce and terrifying, even, than the largest eagle. And I've heard the same story since, but never yet come across anyone who could actually claim to have seen it happen. Genuine confusion may be to blame: ravens would certainly hang around flocks during lambing, hoping to make a meal of the sickly ones who don't survive, and they may also be attracted to sheep by the prospect of feeding on the invertebrates to be found on their fleeces, and around the animals' dung.

What is clear is that these are formidably intelligent creatures. Not for nothing did Odin choose ravens as his spies and messengers. More than one birder has told me that they're quite capable of counting well past twenty. As we've seen, most birds can be fooled by two people going into a hide, then one leaving – the bird assumes both have gone, and starts to approach the hide much more closely than it would if it thought the hide were occupied. With ravens, you need a lot more people: only at around thirty do they really start to lose count.

This intelligence makes relationships in the raven community very complicated. For the most part, pairs hold territory the whole year round, so winter gatherings tend to be of young, unpaired birds. To some extent they're looking out for each other – there's greater safety in numbers, and the more eyes available, the better the chances of spotting food. In fact, young ravens often call in other ravens once they spot a carcass, hoping to use weight of numbers to deter the resident pair, if there is one, as well as rival scavengers. On the other hand, all those untapped sexual urges, combined with a fierce intellect, means that the young birds are constantly looking to outdo each other in a bid to impress the opposite sex and join the breeding population. It's like a vast, airborne version of *The Only Way is Essex*. Almost.

Studies, including one from the University of Vienna, have suggested that ravens are sensitive to the emotions of the other birds in their flock; for instance, bystanders appeared to attempt to relieve and console the distress of ravens that had just lost fights with fellow flock-members. The benefits are obvious: resolving conflict, and avoiding future dust-ups, maintains relationships that are mutually beneficial. It all sounds intriguingly close to the sort of thing you see in primate societies.

And that, I realise, is what I'm seeing unfold before me. The hundreds of birds congregating are hoping that by banding together, they'll stand a much better chance of making it through the winter. Ravens don't have too many predators to fear – their size puts off most attackers, and their aerial agility enables them to evade others, even including peregrines – but raptors will certainly be deterred by the prospect of plunging into the midst of dozens of stabbing bills. More importantly, put all those highly intelligent minds together, and there's an improved chance that they'll find and exploit more and better food sources.

Quite how they communicate this information to each other isn't clear (and it happens in some other bird species, such as gulls). It could be that some birds simply follow others – the ones that look well fed and generally successful – away from the roost in the morning, and certainly there's evidence of a hierarchy within the flock, just as with other species, with older, more experienced birds taking up residence on the flock's inside, and the newcomers and less successful hanging around the edges. But so important is this gathering to the birds, given the distance they're flying to reach it, that it has to be probable they have other ways of communicating the vital information to each other. It could be by actions – a raven's equivalent of a bee's waggle-dance – or it could be by, effectively, talking to each other.

As I watch, this feels more and more likely. Because, as more and more birds accumulate, their croaking rises to a crescendo of sound, in which, if you listen hard, you can just about pick out the individual 'hrafns', as the birds name themselves again and again.

In the morning, this will all happen in reverse. A growing clamour from long before the first rays of the sun seep over the mountains, then a few coal-black offcuts of night thrown to the wind, and finally the moment when the centrifugal force that binds the whole gathering together is too weak to hold and every remaining bird is scattered and dissolved into the cold, bright day.

It's easy to understand why ravens have inspired such awe, respect and fear down the centuries; and it's not just that these are powerful birds, capable of killing or at the very least of unmaking a body – human or animal – within minutes. It's that they have been our constant companions since the earliest times – as harbingers, as gods, or their confidants, as waste-disposal units, as pests – and yet they're still stubbornly themselves, unfathomable even with the technology and countless hours of research at our disposal.

The light is almost gone now. The wind and the effort of staring into the dying light is making my eyes water, and when they clear a little I can't tell if the dance of pale shapes in the distance is a late convoy of gulls heading up the strait or just the passage of blood cells across my retina. The sky is dark enough that it's impossible to see the approach of individual ravens. I know they're there only because they can't help announcing themselves, but only when one or two of the birds wheel across a thin sliver of paler blue between two cloud banks do they become recognisable. Then they're lost again, little slicks of the purest black clotting the tallest branches of the pines.

12 A Blizzard of Wings

The two pristine white birds flying powerfully in from the north are utterly familiar. Long-necked, long-winged for that matter – most toddlers would be able to put a name to them, as well as reel off that old warning about the birds being able to break your arm if angered.

Swans. Until the recent colonisation of these islands by the little egret, and the even more recent return of the spoonbill, any large white bird in the wild could be confidently identified as a swan, even at extreme distance, by birder and 'civilian' alike.

But taking a longer, closer look, I know it's not quite as straightforward as that. There's something more compact about this pair, and as they pass almost directly overhead, I can see their bills are yellow and black, and lack the prominent knobbly protrusion of the orange beak of the mute swan – the species familiar to all of us everywhere, from city park to remote Scottish loch. There isn't the wing noise – a creaking, far-carrying throb – that so often gives away the presence of the latter either, although there's the brief susurration of feathers swishing through cold winter air.

And there is, suddenly and wonderfully, a bright, trumpeting 'kloo-kloo-kloo' from each of them, a clarion call to their fellow travellers, somewhere behind them on a wind straight out of the Arctic. These are whooper swans, and they arrive like the first snows of winter, a few brief flurries followed by a steady and thickening blizzard, their whiteness all the more startling in its complete contrast to the washed-out earth tones of the bleak fenlands around them.

And sure enough, the snowstorm isn't far behind those first few flakes. The sky is blank and featureless. It's too grey for actual snow, although it feels more than cold enough, and there's a thin, mizzly gauze that dulls and blurs the muted colours of the countryside even more; but from somewhere away to the north comes a distant honking noise, not unlike a toy trumpet, which increases in volume until a long, strung-out straggle of birds emerges from the mist.

There'll be time enough to count them later, so for the moment I simply enjoy watching them arrive. They take a sweeping curve around behind the visitor centre, and then they drop abruptly down towards earth – a manoeuvre known as 'wiffling' – and there's the faraway sound of tired bodies splashing into the welcoming water of the Ouse Washes. The trumpeting, meanwhile, continues at the same volume and pitch, but now it takes on an affably triumphal air. It's a fanfare for a difficult, dangerous journey accomplished against all sorts of odds, and it's hard not to want to join in by shouting in celebration yourself.

These whoopers, like most of their species who spend their winters in Britain, have arrived from Iceland, although a few birds from the Russian and Fenno-Scandian breeding populations may make their way here too. At least three-quarters of the Icelandic birds – perhaps 15,000 in total – head south each autumn, and from September through to the end of November they make the journey of at least 600 miles in a single flight, and start dropping in to their wintering grounds. These include much of Ireland, the Severn estuary, Morecambe Bay, the Solway Firth, and a host of locations in Northumberland and Scotland.

Nowhere else are they quite so concentrated, and so easy to see at relatively close quarters, as here, in the seemingly unpromising surroundings of one of the most intensively farmed areas of Britain. At the RSPB's Ouse Washes reserve, and even more so at the Wildfowl & Wetlands Trust's nearby Welney reserve, large flocks can be seen throughout the winter. And there's always the chance of further arrivals: harsh weather back in the land of ice and fire can change the minds of stay-behind birds and send them arrowing towards East Anglia as well.

The Ouse Washes are part of the flood management scheme that transformed a former wilderness into an agricultural paradise. As the Ouse, and a little further north, the Nene, emerge from the rolling hills of the Midlands and start to cross the flatlands of Cambridgeshire, they're transformed from meandering ribbons, narrowed by reeds or widened by pools, to uniformly wide, dead-straight canals, rivers shaped and harnessed to man's purpose. That said, perhaps they're merely trained, rather than tamed, because every winter, as the waters flow off the clay and ironstone hills of the English Midlands, the Ouse and the Nene and the Welland reassert themselves and remind us that they are not to be trifled with. On my own drive to work, across Leicestershire and Rutland, a few days of rain is enough to turn the wide valley between Caldecott and Duddington into a myriad of little lakes and pools, brimful of wigeon, teal and other wildfowl. Further downstream, past Peterborough and Whittlesey, the result is even more spectacular, and the rivers spill out onto the fields widely and seemingly wildly.

Except it's not really wild. It's a trade-off. When the Fens were drained, men were sensible enough to realise that in winter it would be impossible to wholly restrain the run-off of a huge part of central England, so they built sluices and drains and channels that would enable them to inundate the land close to the rivers in a controlled fashion. These are the Washes. Even in summer, they can be very damp and largely given over to grazing rather than arable farming, but in winter and spring they revert to the genuine wetland they once were. And, as you might imagine, that attracts a lot of birds, especially waders and wildfowl.

In a place such as Welney, whooper swans look perfectly at home. The changed landscape – a vast sky-mirror broken here and there by trees and power lines, virtually the only feature to betray a human presence – doesn't look so different from the birds' summer home in Iceland. It's flatter, certainly, but the earth, where it can be seen, has the same black hue, albeit thanks to the high peat content rather than volcanic ash. However, these swans are actually Johnny-come-latelies, who only really started to arrive in great numbers in the 1980s, the reserve having been created way back in 1968. At that time, it was already known as a major wintering area for their close relative, the smaller, more delicate-looking Bewick's swan, which arrives from the Arctic regions of Scandinavia and Russia – but the whoopers knew a good thing when they saw it.

For a start, both Welney and the RSPB reserve sit in the middle of an immense arable area, which means that fields full of winter wheat, potatoes and sugar beet are never far away. On top of which, these wildlife sanctuaries offer somewhere for large numbers of these big, conspicuous birds to roost safely. Finally, to cap it all off, the Wildfowl & Wetlands Trust soon started feeding the swans and other wildfowl, reducing the birds' need to forage far and wide.

Feeding the birds might seem like cheating when it comes to attracting two species so emblematic of the wild northern wastes, but the activity has a dual purpose. On the one hand, it does ensure that the birds don't go hungry even during the hardest winter weather, and as such it's only a larger-scale version of what so many of us do at home, filling up the feeders so that our favourite robin or blackbird makes it through another year. On the other hand, it also removes any need for the swans to go roving too far in search of sustenance, something that could bring them to grief on one of the aforementioned power lines (although precautions such as high-visibility discs on the wires have reduced deaths greatly), as well as into conflict with the farmers of Cambridgeshire and Norfolk. While they're hoovering up unwanted beet tops, or picking through stubble, they're a picturesque and evocative addition to any farming scene, but even a relatively small flock of whoopers or Bewick's can do a great deal of damage to a crop that's still in the ground.

Welney's whoopers, then, and Bewick's swans for that matter, are prime examples of species that have taken full advantage of the opportunities that man has offered them, both intentionally and inadvertently. There can be around 2,000 of the former and 5,000 of the latter present in this area at the height of winter, turning the dull watercolours of the Washes into a shimmering snowfield that is testament to the conservation efforts of several organisations – and one man in particular.

Sir Peter Scott was the son of a British hero – the tragic polar explorer Captain Robert Falcon Scott – who became one himself, albeit for quite different reasons. Indeed, the roots of Sir Peter's entire life's work can be found in his father's last, poignant letter to his wife, written as he awaited death in a tent just eleven miles from safety in a ten-day Antarctic blizzard. 'Make the boy interested in natural history if you can; it is better than games,' he advised.

The boy, Peter, was just two years old at the time, but over the next seventy-eight years he was to become arguably the most influential British conservationist and ornithologist of the twentieth century, not to mention a major figure in both fields internationally. After serving in the Royal Navy in the Second World War, and unsuccessfully standing as a Conservative candidate in the 1945 general election, Peter Scott founded the Severn Wildfowl Trust at Slimbridge, Gloucestershire, close to where the wide waters of the River Severn open out into the Bristol Channel – some of the richest and most important wintering grounds for waders and wildfowl in Europe.

One of his early successes was saving the nene, or Hawaiian goose, from extinction by means of a captive-breeding programme, a technique that has since been used successfully with a number of other threatened species. He would go on to help found the World Wide Fund for Nature and carry out ornithological work that has shaped conservation around the world; but his most lasting legacy is here in the UK. The Severn Wildfowl Trust became the Wildfowl & Wetlands Trust, with nine large reserves across the UK, including at Welney, although Slimbridge remains the heart of everything it does, indelibly associated with Scott and his work.

This included, in 1964, deducing that each Bewick's swan has an absolutely unique pattern of yellow and black markings on its bill, enabling scientists to easily identify individual birds from one year to the next. Scott actually painted little mugshots of each bird, and gave them names, initiating one of the longest-running wildlife studies in the world. This has enabled the WWT to keep a very close eye on how the birds are doing on a wider scale.

As with most species, numbers across Europe have fluctuated over a long period, but in the mid-1990s there were thought to be around 30,000 birds in total. A 2010 survey, however, showed as few as 18,000 left, with power lines, poisoning from lead shot, and illegal hunting blamed for the dramatic decline. In Britain, too, numbers have declined, although they vary anyway according to the weather. In colder winters, more swans are forced this far west, but in milder years, many stop short and spend the winter in the Netherlands, or even further east.

Whoopers, on the other hand, are doing pretty well on a world scale, and back at Welney they've become the unwitting but obliging stars of one of Britain's greatest wildlife shows. Only a couple of weeks after watching those first birds arrive, I'm back there on a clear, frosty afternoon as the sun starts to sink below the horizon.

The hide at Welney is unlike practically any other in British birdwatching. It's a heated observatory with plenty of seating, and a glass front that affords views right out across the sea that is, for at least part of the year, the fields of Cambridgeshire and Norfolk. Accordingly, it has attracted a quite different gathering from what you might expect to find in the typically draughty, creaky, glorified garden shed that is the average hide. There's a scattering of obvious birdwatchers, for certain, including three or four hefting huge zoom lenses on their Nikons and Canons, and others with tell-tale spotting scopes, but at least 75 per cent of the people present show no signs of being fully in the throes of a birdwatching addiction. If they have binoculars – and far from all of them do – these tend to be one of two kinds: either chunky, passed-down-from-granddad ex-forces types, or compact, pocket-sized models as sold at special offer price in certain national newspapers. There's a heartening range of ages, from five to at least eighty-five, and a high number of families.

The light has faded. The natural light that is, because outside the observatory huge floodlights (appropriately enough) are now illuminating the wide waters, silhouetting a group of pochards, with their distinctively pointy-headed outline, and a loose flock of bickering mallards. Here and there a black-tailed godwit stands hunched, as if pondering whether to continue feeding under this artificial daylight, or to fly off to somewhere quieter and darker. And swans are gathering, slowly but steadily, in a 180-degree arc around the great glass window. Some fly in from a day spent gleaning whatever sustenance they can find from the surrounding fields, and arrive with a showy splashdown. Others, given the numbers involved, must be swimming in via unseen channels and creeks, having already spent some of the day on the reserve. Next to the smaller, duller ducks and waders, they appear both much bigger and much more real, their whiteness giving them a cleaner, sharper outline than the grey and brown birds around them. Only here and there is a swan still muddied by the day's exertions, the grubby stains on their plumage threatening to relegate them, if only temporarily, from the divine to the profane.

Inside the observatory, there's a hum of expectation that creates an atmosphere in itself. It's welcome, because although there're lots of good things to be said for a hide designed with the watchers' comfort in mind, one downside is that it appears to have shut out the noise of the birds themselves. Not just that of the swans, but the exhilarating whistle of the many wigeon bobbing somewhere just beyond the floodlights' reach, and the mixed clamour of every other bird sounding off before the long silence of the fenland night. Every now and then, as a door opens somewhere behind us, we catch a snatch of their voices raised to the winter stars, letting a little bit of the northern wilderness creep back into us.

Now any football or rugby fan will tell you that there's something very special about a floodlit match: it's to do, of course, with the smell of the damp, cold night air mixed with cigarette smoke and the heady aromas of meat pies, beer and Bovril; but it's also a lot to do with the way the lights create a little illuminated block in which you, the other spectators and the players are trapped for ninety minutes or so, with the whole of the outside world reduced to a dull, shadowy blur.

And that's what happens. In daylight, even if we were similarly waiting for a particular natural spectacle to begin, we'd be scanning the landscape and skies beyond the reserve, hoping to turn up something unexpected or unusual. Here, we have no choice but to focus on the relatively small stage before us, expectant but not impatient to know what's about to unfold. It ought to feel restrictive, but it's not. It's liberating, in fact, to know that you can concentrate your whole attention solidly on a single phenomenon.

As I sit there, it even strikes me that perhaps those among us without binoculars might have a point. Raise a pair of modern optics to your eyes and you can be astounded by the pin-sharpness of the image, and by how natural the colour is, and yet, no matter how advanced the binoculars are, how wide the field of view, you'll still find your view circumscribed to a relatively narrow tunnel of vision. Outside it, anything can – and probably is – happening. For once, the naked eye might be the better bet, allowing you to take in the whole scope of what's going on.

There's movement outside. A WWT employee is padding around in front of the observatory, carrying a huge bucket. He stops and dips a large scoop into it, then flings corn out onto the dark waters. Within seconds the loose smattering of drifting floes has been consolidated into a single huge iceberg that dwarfs the darker shapes of the mallards and pochards around them. Long necks lunge towards the floating grain to snaffle it before it sinks, and although there's plenty to go round, there's all the squabbling and bickering that you might expect from hundreds and hundreds of large, hungry birds who know how hard even an East Anglian winter can be.

It's a curiously domestic-looking scene, rather like farmyard geese being fed, only on a much larger and grander scale; and yet every time a head turns and there's a flash of tell-tale yellow and black on the bill, you're reminded that these birds spend half their year in the remotest, bleakest parts of the Arctic; and a little shiver runs down your spine, in recognition of their utter wildness, as well, maybe, as in sympathy for what they must go through.

That duality to their nature is, I think, what keeps me and hundreds of other birdwatchers coming back to Welney year after year. Whooper and Bewick's swans seem to encompass the entire range of the birdwatching experience within the great arcs of their migratory flights. Their whiteness is a blank screen onto which any of us can project our own motivations for birding, from the thrill of seeing rare and scarce creatures in their natural habitat, to the simple pleasure, originating right back in childhood, of seeing waterbirds being fed.

And the swans carry so much with them on their long flights out of the north. Not only the glamour, exoticism and romance of coming from places most of us will never visit, but scientific considerations as well. Like most migratory birds, they're the bearers of messages on the state of the planet; in the case of the Bewick's swans, rather worrying messages that speak of deforestation and habitat degradation in Siberia.

For now, the swans keep on coming and going, until they've all had their fill of the food being scattered, and one or two watchers slip out of the observatory; but for the most part we remain transfixed by this strange sight until the last of the birds drifts away across the water to take up its roosting place for the night.

Back in the car, I have a long drive ahead of me. I'm travelling down a long, straight stretch alongside one of the 'cuts' or 'drains' that criss-cross the flatlands, and as the moon emerges from behind cloud, it picks out two large white shapes tucked in to the far bank. Mute swans. The wind ruffles the feathers of their wings and backs for a moment, like a breeze whipping up little whirlwinds of snow, but they sail on, oblivious to weather and passing traffic, seeming more wild and remote than even their migratory cousins did earlier in the evening.

Swans occupy a prominent place in our culture. In part, this is down to their historical status as royal birds. The Crown was considered to own every swan, although nobles and gentry might be granted local ownership rights too, and certainly carried out the day-to-day management of the population. And, although monarchs no doubt valued these birds for their ornamental value – what estate isn't enhanced by their graceful presence? – the main reason they were guarded so jealously was that they formed the centrepieces of many a banquet.

There's a temptation in Britain to ascribe most legislation conferring ownership of wild animals and birds on the upper echelons of society to the Normans – certainly they introduced the hated forest laws, which prevented peasants from hunting not only deer, but more modest game, such as rabbits. Where swans are concerned, however, the process had started well before 1066 and the arrival of William the Bastard, as his English subjects were wont to call him. A century earlier, in 966, King Edgar had granted the monks of Crowland Abbey rights over the resident swans (the abbey being a short flight away from those mute swans I watched floating on the drain), and the laws and customs regarding the birds may have accumulated over the next few hundred years until, in 1482, they started to be formalised into what were known as the swan laws. Swans were expensive to raise, and their meat was a highly valued delicacy, so there were harsh penalties for anyone caught interfering with them or their eggs. They continued to be the table item of highest prestige until the seventeenth century saw the introduction of the cheaper and easier-to-handle turkey from the New World.

But vestiges of our former swan culture – or should that be industry – still remain. Every July, a stretch of the Thames sees 'swan-upping', in which the Queen's Swan Marker and the representatives of the Vintners and Dyers livery companies catch and mark as many swans as possible; and at Abbotsbury in Dorset, hundreds of mute swans inhabit the same site that their kind has occupied for at least 700 years, having originally been kept by the monks of the local abbey.

All this might help explain why swans figure so prominently in the names and signs of pubs. They were a familiar, aesthetically pleasing and easily recognisable image; they had an aspirational quality (while dining on lesser fare in the hostelry, you could imagine yourself at a royal feast); and perhaps most importantly of all, they were regularly used in heraldry. Thus a landlord might have the swan as his sign to curry favour with, or show affiliation to, a particular member of the local gentry.

But history is only part of the story. The British mute swan population of 45,000 or so adults is around half the European total, and at least part of their success here is due to the location. Like the whoopers and Bewick's, these are essentially northern birds, so our cool but largely benevolent climate suits them down to the ground. It's only when you birdwatch outside Britain that you realise just how favoured we are. In the rest of Europe, mute swans are thinly scattered and sometimes hard to find. Even further afield, the black-necked swan of South America and the black swan of Australasia have their own charm, but somehow feel second best. When the British say 'swan', we mean something huge and snow-white – part-angel, part-apparition, part-domestic animal.

Along with the truly wild swans, the whoopers and Bewick's, mute swans have left their mark on the wider culture of Europe. From Greek myth, in which Helen of Troy was conceived as a result of a union between the Queen of Sparta and Zeus, disguised as a swan, through to Wagner's operas *Lohengrin* and *Parsifal*, both of which draw on Norse myths involving swan-maidens, the birds have been an inspiration to artists, writers and composers, symbolising beauty, as well as love and fidelity, because of their habit of mating for life.

And then there's the enduring story of the 'swan song', a phrase that has passed into much more general usage to mean a person's last act or performance. Chaucer and Shakespeare both mention the original, literal version: the belief that swans sing a song just before dying, having previously been silent.

It seems to have some basis in truth, at least where the whooper and Bewick's swans are concerned, as both have been known to issue a series of long drawn-out musical notes as their lungs collapse before the moment of death. But neither, of course, are silent throughout their lives, so perhaps somewhere along the line there was some confusion with their mute cousins. However, even mute swans hiss and grunt extensively when the mood takes them, so perhaps the myth is the result of good old poetic licence, and the understandable desire to make a story better than it really is.

Ten days after visiting Welney, I'm on my way up to Edinburgh from Newcastle. It's a journey I've made many times, and although there are frustrations aplenty on the single-carriageway stretches of the A1 between Newcastle and the border, there are compensations for the birdwatcher. Slightly dangerous compensations, because they can turn what should be a drive of ninety minutes or so into an all-day affair ...

I manage to resist the urge to turn off the road shortly after passing Morpeth and trawl the many small reserves along Druridge Bay for unusual migrant waders. These sites, most of them former industrial workings, can look distinctly unpromising at first glance, but they have an astonishing roll of honour to their credit, including the much-disputed record of a slender-billed curlew sighting in 1998, which if genuine would be one of the last good sightings of a species now possibly extinct. The slender-billed curlew once bred in the vast, still partially unmapped taiga of Siberia, and used to be a regular winter visitor around the Mediterranean, until hunting and habitat degradation sent numbers into a down-curve not unlike that of the bird's own bill: steady and regular, but growing more and more exaggerated. A final concerted scientific effort to find the last remaining birds took place during the last decade but met with no confirmed success, merely a handful of intriguing and far-flung possibilities: a sketch of an unusual wader from Andalusia; unfamiliar calls from overflying birds in eastern Europe. And the Druridge Bay bird? In recent years the British Birds Rarities Committee and the British Ornithologists' Union Records Committee have reconsidered the sighting and removed it from the British List. But that doesn't mean it wasn't a slender-billed curlew, and there are scores if not hundreds of British birders who will go to their graves convinced they saw one of the last hurrahs of a tragically doomed species.

I digress, but this stretch of coast has that effect on you. Even after you've overcome the temptations of Druridge, there are the harbours and estuaries to consider, such as Alnmouth and Seahouses, where in winter the eiders crowd, oohing and aahing like so many pensioners catching up on a week's news. And there's the history. This was once the Anglo-Saxon kingdom of Bernicia, one of the two main constituent parts of Northumbria, and here more than in most parts of England the pre-Conquest past is still there to be seen. Up in the dark hills, there's Yeavering Bell, where archaeological digs have uncovered the sort of royal hall that you can imagine *Beowulf* being recited in – that you can imagine the story of *Beowulf* taking place in, in fact.

On the coast, there's Bamburgh Castle perched dramatically atop its rock, no less impressive now, as a Victorian rebuild, than it was through the medieval period, when it guarded against Viking and Scottish invasions (not always successfully), and played its part in internecine struggles such as the Wars of the Roses. Beyond it, I catch glimpses of the causeway curving out to Lindisfarne. The castle there, too, is more nineteenth-century reconstruction than original, but it's not difficult to picture things as they once were, with the monastery that was one of the cradles of English Christianity rising above the tidal island.

But no. I resist this too, and drive on towards the border with thoughts of reaching Auld Reekie in time to take a daylight stroll. A skein of pink-footed geese arrows over at one stage, returning to their roost on the coast after a day foraging on the hills, but I don't follow. And then, just when the danger seems over, I'm ambushed.

I turn off to go into Berwick for petrol just as the sun starts to touch the Cheviot tops, spilling a warm, golden wash over the town, and as I drive across the high bridge over the widening Tweed, I glance sideways to be met by an extraordinary sight. For a moment it looks like a scene from a documentary on Alaska or Canada, where ice-floes crowd some Arctic river, and bears and bald eagles hunt salmon. There are still salmon in the Tweed, but here the bald eagles are replaced by cormorants. And the ice-floes? The ice-floes are hundreds of mute swans, clustered on the estuary in little huddles that gather and disperse, gather and disperse, at the command of invisible, unfathomable forces.

I stop in town, and walk back to the bridge to spend half an hour watching this strange gathering. Strange because mute swans are so legendarily territorial. While the old story about them breaking arms might be an exaggeration, they're often willing to vigorously attack anything they see as a threat. In this case, it turns out that they're willing to put aside rivalries, at least for part of the year, because the estuary of the Tweed provides the perfect safe environment, in late summer and early autumn, in which they can moult, which is to say replace part of their plumage, including their flight feathers. During such a time, the birds are of course more vulnerable, so a safe haven is a must. Later in the year, these normally freshwater birds take advantage of the seaweeds and algae that can be found where the river meets the salt waters – like all British estuaries, the Tweed remains free of ice during even the hardest winter.

Even as I watch, a couple of small flotillas nose their way in from the North Sea. There's always something strange about seeing the birds of your local park out on the ocean, and if anything the effect is amplified by the swans' size and obviousness.

The birds stay to feed and grow their new plumage in this peaceful spot. Some birds, up to two hundred non-breeders and juveniles, remain all year, but up to six hundred more birds arrive from late summer onwards from their breeding sites all over Northumberland and the Borders region. Quite why the Tweed is so much more attractive than other estuaries isn't clear. The town has historical connections to royalty, both English and Scottish, so it's possible that there was a certain amount of swan husbandry in the past, building up the core of the modern herd. Having said that, the large numbers seen today seem to have developed from the middle of the twentieth century, so perhaps Berwick just boasts a perfect combination of circumstances for the discerning mute swan.

Whatever the reason, they're a glorious surprise to even the experienced birdwatcher, a perfect example of how even the most everyday (and partially domesticated) of birds takes on a whole new character when seen in a different context, or much greater numbers than usual, or both.

I drive on towards night and a new country, my mind swept clean by the white wings of this sudden snowstorm.

Parrots, Pests and
Garrulous Bohemians

Learning to recognise the silhouettes of different species is a
key part of becoming a birdwatcher, especially if a lot of your
birding is of the casual variety – snatched moments in between
chores and errands and appointments and the diary-clutter of
modern life. Your binoculars might not be to hand. The light
might be poor. You might, as I am now, be standing in the
car park of your local branch of Lidl, cradling an armful of
discounted comestibles while rummaging through your trouser
pocket for the car keys.

Just beyond the end of the car park, where the land slopes
away towards the bypass, there's a single, moderately large
passerine in the top of a bare rowan tree. It's a sad comment on
the population status of the fast-declining starling that I am,
to begin with, delighted to see one of the speckled, strutting
mimics so close to home. Just recently, they've been hard to
find away from a few regular roost sites.

However, when the bird shifts slightly, its head is clearly
visible against the ice-blue sky beyond, and my heart starts to
race a little. The general shape and size are right for starling,
true, but what's that rather chunky crest doing jabbing jauntily
towards the daylight moon? I'm pretty sure I know what I'm
seeing, but I inch my way round my car anyway, closer, closer,
until a little more detail becomes visible. Yellow fringes to a
wing flashed with white, and a yellow tip to the tail. I think
I can see a few droplets of red on the wing, too, but maybe
they're just rowan berries on one of the nearer branches. No

matter. This is a waxwing, so-called because those red feather-tips on the wings were once thought to resemble sealing wax. It's a gorgeous creature, colourful without being gaudy, and I silently curse the fact that I left my binoculars at home, but it's still a pleasure to stand and watch it here, half a mile from my home.

Such a pleasure that I lose all track of time. After a few minutes, my hands are so cold that I don't notice I'm losing grip on a jar of strawberry jam, which slips from my grasp and smashes on the tarmac. The waxwing, predictably, takes fright and flight.

The smashed jar poses a dilemma. I really, really want that jam – what else am I going to have on my toast tomorrow morning? But I can't face the embarrassment of walking straight back into the same shop, to the same, lone cashier, to buy exactly the same thing. A man has to have some self-respect.

This is where the recent diversification of the British supermarket sector pays unexpected dividends. Just across the road, there's a branch of Lidl's rival, Aldi. I sheepishly climb into the car, edge out of one car park, and straight into another. As I climb out of the car again, I catch movement in the line of small rowan trees planted in the bay-dividers. A sudden flurry of movement, in which berries and waxed-look wingtips become one and the same. There's a flock of perhaps sixty waxwings, moving through the trees, methodically stripping off the remaining rather shrivelled fruits, and gorging on them. There's a certain amount of chattering from the excited birds – the second part of their scientific name *Bombycilla garrulus* refers to this noisy jabbering – but for the most part they give their meal their full attention. It's the avian equivalent of a swarm of locusts. Once they've finished here, they'll be straight off in search of their next meal – yet no one seems to be watching them but me.

Well, me and a mistle thrush. This large, powerful-looking songbird, famously so unfazed by extreme winter weather that it was known as the stormcock in centuries past, is watching with mounting fury as the invaders loot one of the food sources that might have seen it through the darkest, coldest months. From a nearby hawthorn hedge, it makes a sound like one of those football rattles you see on newsreel clips of 1950s FA Cup Finals, occasionally making a darting flight towards the waxwings. Each time, a few of them take flight, their wings making their own clattering noise as if in echo or mockery of the thrush's alarm call; then they circle in a loose flock before returning to the rowans. They're not about to be deterred by any single thrush, let alone a butter-fingered buffoon in a fleece.

My hands become cold again, but I just can't drag myself away from these glorious creatures. This time, even without binoculars, I can make out all those beautiful details on the wings and tails, but there's more. The black eye-stripe and 'beard' gives them a bandit look that, as that mistle thrush might tell you, isn't wholly inappropriate, while the orangey-red blush under the tail and around the forehead and cheeks is the leaves of vast Siberian forests brought out of the mysterious east. So, I stand until the last shades of yellow and pink disappear from the western sky, the car park empties of vehicles, and I hear the shop doors being locked somewhere behind me.

I never do get that jam.

Even a single waxwing is a truly wonderful thing to behold, an exquisite little miniature, a masterpiece of fine detail. But an equally important part of their appeal to any birdwatcher is what they represent, and the twin auras of exoticism and adventure they carry.

Waxwings come to us from Siberia, as well as European Russia and Scandinavia (although their full name is Bohemian waxwing, this refers to their general foreignness, rather than any actual connection to central Europe). When they arrive in Britain, it's at the end of an odyssey that takes them across thousands of miles, including the cold and inhospitable North Sea. These invasions, or irruptions, to use the correct term, are triggered by a lack of suitable food in their home territories; the very cold, snowy winters there would make movement south necessary anyway, but if the nearest mild wintering areas have had a bad berry crop, or are colder and snowier than usual, then the birds have to set their sights much further afield.

Sometimes – most years, in fact – they'll find what they seek en route through Europe, dropping off flock after flock as they go, until what reaches us is a thin trickle of birds that don't get far past our north-east coasts. But there are years when even eastern, central, and finally the near edge of western Europe are all having their own bad weather, or have had poor berry crops, and so the birds keep on going, giving the UK what's become known as a waxwing winter.

These winters generally happen every four or five years. Trees and bushes don't produce the same harvest every year. Warm, wet springs mean that a lot of fruit and seeds are produced the following autumn, which in turn means that more of the birds that eat these foods can survive through the winter. If the following spring is cold and dry, that year's berry and seed yield will be proportionally lower, yet will have to feed an increased population. It's a complex equation that, ultimately, always comes up with the same simple answer: at least some birds must move, or die.

So, usually around the end of October, there comes a day when a report arrives of a small group of waxwings in some coastal town such as Whitley Bay or Scarborough. And, when that happens, birders around the country shift nervously in their chairs in office buildings and business parks, or scan the skies for compact, starling-like flocks as they pause at traffic lights. Over the succeeding days, more waxwings will start to pop up along the coast, anywhere from Fraserburgh to Felixstowe. This is when things grow really tense for the average British birdwatcher. There's a nervous pause, a collective held breath, as the voracious visitors strip the berry trees of their chosen out-of-season resort. Are they the overspill from an avian tide that has largely spent its force on the near-continent? Or are they the scouts for a vast invasion force, outriders of a constantly moving horde of insatiable fruit-guzzlers?

Thankfully, it doesn't take long to find out. Those original birds move on to find their next food source, but in a good waxwing year they'll quickly be forgotten about as larger and larger flocks make landfall along the east coast, before the invaders start to make their way south and west, leapfrogging each other in their search for sustenance. By the end of November, they can be found pretty much everywhere, and their nomadic gluttony will continue well into the spring.

They're not the only species to perform these irruptions, by any means. Bramblings, crossbills, and the continental populations of familiar birds such as coal tits all roam far and wide in response to adverse weather or food shortages. What makes waxwings easier to track than these and most migratory birds, for that matter, is their habit of sticking together in single-species flocks, and their liking for habitat that's bizarrely at odds with their exotic appearance. Waxwings, you see, love car parks.

They're not restricted to them, obviously, being birds of the Siberian taiga at heart, but the fact is that, in most of the UK, the best place to look for berries is often in the middle of a town or city, between serried rows of vehicles. That's because car parks – and especially supermarket and hospital car parks – tend to be built to much the same pattern the country over. At least some of the bays will be divided by small flower beds and, as well as rowan trees, shrubs such as cotoneaster, pyracantha and guelder rose are favoured. All produce exactly the sort of berries that waxwings love, and so on a given winter's day it's possible to watch one of our great wildlife spectacles unfold a few yards away from the irritable, irritating crush of the Christmas shopping rush. In fact, that's partly *why* it's one of our greatest wildlife spectacles: no other juxtaposes untamed, wild nature and crass commercialism, the sublime and the ridiculous, quite so closely.

There's also the fact that you never quite know what you're going to get when you stumble across a flock of waxwings. They are usually rather nervous birds, but their need for large amounts of food, fast, can lead them to throw off their natural caution and approach humans closely. An apple impaled on a stick has been known to be enough to lure them down into a garden, to within touching distance.

Once they've gorged themselves on fruit, they can become distinctly sluggish, intoxicated, in fact. A diet consisting entirely of sugary berries might be thought to be asking for trouble, and because the berries are generally low in most nutrients, they have to be eaten in very large quantities – often more than double the bird's weight in a day. Waxwings do have large livers, and can actually metabolise ethanol better than humans, but nonetheless there are instances of the birds becoming drunk on the fermenting fruit in their stomachs and coming to ruin as a result, flying into buildings and cars, or being picked off by grateful predators. More commonly, they merely appear rather sluggish, and remarkably tame. Like all the best drunks, they're your best mate, honest.

Waxwings and their will-they, won't-they routine are an essential part of the birdwatching year and, in a good year, most parts of Britain stand a reasonable chance of playing host to their flocks.

Other exotic visitors are rather harder to find, either because of their shy and retiring nature, or because they have, as yet, tended to remain within a few relatively small parts of these islands. It could be said that they're no longer truly visitors, having long since made the move permanent. But I'm not talking about birds that have naturally colonised Britain, whether as a result of a warming climate or because of other factors, such as habitat change, which invite an extension of their range. Little egrets would be the prime example of this category of bird. Only twenty-five years ago seeing one would have triggered a twitch of nationwide proportions, but these days it's possible to see dozens at any sizeable water body, south of the Humber, at least. Indeed, go to a suitable roost site, such as the National Wetland Centre, Llanelli, and you can watch the banks of the Burry Inlet turn snow-white in high summer as the elegant invaders arrive for the night.

They won't be the last incomers, either. Two close relatives, the larger great white egret and the smaller but gregarious cattle egret, have arrived in ever-increasing numbers in recent years, along with night herons and little bitterns. It might seem paradoxical that herons and egrets are pursuing their expansion plans with such unbridled enthusiasm at a time when we're being told that our wetland habitats are in danger of disappearing entirely, but in fact there's no logical disconnect. The more specialist birds, such as the little bittern, have tended to drop in at reserves, while the more generalist species – step forward, the cattle egret – are far from tied to actual wetland. A damp field full of sheep or, as their name suggests, cows, is all the encouragement they need.

No, I'm thinking instead of a couple of species that have grasped the inadvertent helping hand offered them by man, and almost bitten it off. Both are capable of adding a swatch of colour to the dullest of late autumn days, but both, as you'll see, are capable of arousing suspicion and even hostility. Both, in the weeks after my waxwing encounter, cross my path when I least expect it …

I'm walking in a large but little-watched reserve a couple of miles from home one morning, kicking my way through drifts of oak leaves and generally enjoying the colours and smells of a deciduous wood as winter sets in. I've already seen green and great spotted woodpeckers bouncing between stands of trees, and little flocks of siskins and lesser redpolls performing their casual gymnastics in a small patch of alders. The prospect of a woodcock or two in the main area of oaks is also appealing, and I start walking besides the drystone wall that forms its perimeter, looking for the little gap you can slip through onto one of the main paths.

Just before I reach the gap, there's a point at which a small stream passes through a culvert under the wall. For no particular reason (I've never seen anything there before), I stop and peer over the stones, to where the stream is pooling into little more than a large puddle. And if I'm surprised, then it's fair to say that what momentarily takes me aback gives every impression of being taken just as unawares itself. It's a bird, of course. But, were it not for the fact that it quickly recovers its composure enough to lift from the water and fly away between the trees at speed, I'd be hard pressed to say if it was a thing of flesh and blood or the most astonishing piece of origami ever created.

Mandarin ducks, or the males at least, really need to be seen to be believed. List their features – a bright red bill, a white crescent through and above the eye, brown-red face and long 'whiskers', purple breast, ruddy flanks and two orange 'sails' on its rear – and you get some idea of what an astonishing melange they are. On paper, it shouldn't work, but the male mandarin manages to be both beautiful and dignified in all his oriental finery.

The name comes from the impression created by those chestnut 'whiskers' – not unlike the mandarins of the courts of the Chinese emperors – and in the normal course of things the bird's home area is restricted to China, Taiwan, Japan, a small part of Russia, and the two Koreas. Pretty much across that range, though, it has suffered declines as a result of its particular requirements. Foremost among these is tree cavities for nesting, and when deforestation is the order of the day such nest-holes are at a premium. Except in Japan, where a population of around five thousand pairs remains, mandarins are being slowly squeezed out of their homes.

Which is where Britain comes in. First brought to Britain in the mid-eighteenth century, a pair finally bred at London Zoo in 1834, but it wasn't until nearly a hundred years later that they really started to put down roots. Aviculturist Alfred Ezra kept mandarins as part of his own collection, but also attempted releases in a bid to establish it as a British breeding bird. Escapes from other collections added to the potential breeding stock, to the extent that breeding birds can now be found everywhere from Dorset to north-east Scotland and Northern Ireland. As well as being tree-nesters, mandarins like dense cover around the nest, and bodies of water with plenty of overhanging vegetation, so the lakes and reservoirs of Surrey and Berkshire have been their areas of densest population. At the last count, there were around seven thousand of the birds in the UK.

There are small populations on the Continent, too, with Berlin's city-centre Tiergarten as good a place as any to get really close-up views. If you have to put a label on these birds, then 'feral' fits the bill. They're self-sustaining and supporting (although, like many ducks, they will sometimes overcome their shyness to accept food from man), but they certainly wouldn't have got here naturally.

So I watch this glorious creature disappear at speed between the trees, its aerial agility almost as impressive as its exotic looks. My patch, Charnwood Forest, has long played host to a small population, with flocks of thirty or so occasionally reported from a handful of sites. But I've always found them hard to track down, because perhaps the most remarkable thing of all about the mandarin is just how difficult they can be to spot, even when they're right in front of you sporting their full 'look at me' outfit.

Their predilection for habitats with overhanging greenery contributes to their elusiveness: they'll happily stay tucked in close to the banks the whole time, and the easiest time to see them is often late summer, when falling water levels force them out into the centre of lakes. But by that time, the male has lost some of his finery and resembles his less showy (though still neat and striking) mate.

After coming across the mandarin, a funny thing happens. It happens a lot in birdwatching now I come to think of it.

No sooner do you spot one difficult-to-find bird than they seem to pop up everywhere you look. If you take a moment to think it through, there's really nothing strange about it. For a start, once you've seen a bird in the flesh (or in the feather) you get your eye in – to borrow a cricketing phrase. However good a field guide is, it can't entirely capture the essence of a bird, because it's dealing with them as still lives; but once you see how they move, feed, fly, how their feathers flare or fade according to storm and season, you'll know them when you see them again. And there's a second, perhaps even more important reason: take a memorable and inspiring sighting of any species, and you're immediately subconsciously looking to repeat it again and again, to recapture that initial thrill. This might be a vain hope, of course, but it's an entirely natural and human one.

Just three days after seeing that lone male, I'm visiting friends who live in that borderland where London meets the Home Counties. The area is a curious mixture of the decidedly utilitarian, the tastefully landscaped, and the defiantly natural, with business parks separated from commuter estates by golf courses, heaths and commons and high beech hangers. When we take a long but leisurely Sunday lunchtime walk to the pub, we're accompanied by both the constant tinnitus of the M25 and the distant cawing of rooks.

We're walking along a lane between two smallish lakes when our attention is drawn to a flotilla of birds drifting slowly out from the wooded shore of the nearest lake. Presumably two fishermen setting up on the bank are what has moved them, and as they start to come nearer we can finally see them for what they are.

In low winter sunshine filtering through oaks and beeches the bright and contrasting colours of the males act like the dazzle-pattern used to camouflage First World War warships, rendering them remarkably inconspicuous; but those orange sails on the rears of the males are nevertheless distinctive, giving them a shape irresistibly reminiscent of the sort of paper boats made by children. Mandarins again, in their British stronghold, a stronghold that remains important on a world scale, even though sizeable new populations of the bird have recently been found in China.

We stand and watch as this little squadron, maybe twenty-strong, makes its way towards a small wooded island, seeking out the cover that they love. They're so impossibly ornate, intricately patterned and simply *foreign* that I find myself wondering why everyone in sight – the fishermen, the dog-walkers and the Sunday strollers – isn't standing and staring open-mouthed, or pointing at them in rapt admiration. Maybe people would be if these were the birds of a captive collection, or zoo, but they're effectively just as wild as the blackbirds and robins in the nearby bushes (more so, maybe, given that the latter happily visit gardens to receive free handouts from humans), and as such they go about their business no differently from every other bird out there. If they're special then they certainly don't think so.

And that's what makes them worth seeing again and again. They manage to be jarringly out of place and completely at home, dabbling around the muddy margins with the teal and the mallard. What those other ducks think about these floating pagodas in their midst is anybody's guess, but it's fair to assume that the shock of their appearance has long since worn off.

I've mentioned the ability of birds to transport us in both time and space before – and the experience now, of being carried away to the Far East in the time it takes to whisk up a Yorkshire pudding, would be more than enough for most Sundays. But before my walking companions and I get so much as a whiff of roast potatoes in our nostrils, we're taken on a further Asian detour. It starts with a sparrowhawk, soaring lazily over a copse close to the road. As always this bird provokes panic among the smaller passerines. There's the insistent ticking of a wren, the hysterical warning cackle of a blackbird, and the clatter of woodpigeons' wings as they make their noisy escape.

Then, as we look up in reaction to all the hubbub, the entire top of a beech tree seems to detach itself, with what seemed to be long, thin branches blooming into bright-green leaves in seconds. Ten, twenty, thirty and then some long-tailed, pointed-winged darts flash down towards us, flaring bright green as they catch the sunlight, their 'ak, ak, ak' calls accelerating into a single maelstrom of fear and excitement in perfect harmony with the gathering speed of their escape flight.

Ring-necked parakeets. If mandarins appear like the creation of a designer who just didn't know when to stop, they are at least recognisably ducks, and so perhaps, in the mind of the casual or non-birdwatcher, not all that different from the dabblers at the pond in the park. Parakeets, however, are quite unlike anything native to these islands, with their large, bright-red, hooked bills marking them out unmistakably as members of a family we'd otherwise expect to see in a cage, or perched on a Hollywood pirate's shoulder.

The vividness of their greens and reds, the alien nature of their silhouette, means that your first sight of one above the grey streets of suburban England almost always inspires initial disbelief, turning to joy, chilling into a gnawing fear. Surely, you think, such a wonderfully colourful, elegant creature, a swift sliver of the tropical forest, can't last long in our damp, cold climate? Surely it can only be a matter of time before the mists and gales of a British winter arrive to snuff out this vibrant, verdant bolt from the blue?

That's where appearances can be very deceptive. As a species, the ring-necked (or sometimes, rose-ringed) parakeet is found everywhere from Senegal to Burma, with the subspecies here in Britain being a native of the Indian subcontinent. There, it weathers both the harsh conditions of the Himalayan foothills, as well as rampant deforestation and habitat loss, not to mention air pollution. You'd imagine, after conditions like those, a few squally showers on the Beaconsfield bypass are very little cause for concern.

There are all sorts of rather romantic stories about how parakeets came to be roaming wild in the jungles of the Home Counties, the two favourites being that they were released after being used to give tropical colour to the classic Humphrey Bogart and Katharine Hepburn movie *The African Queen*, partly filmed at Isleworth Studios, Middlesex, in 1951; or that Jimi Hendrix released two on Carnaby Street in 1967.

It would be nice to equate the parakeets with two of the last great stars of the Golden Age of Hollywood, or to think of them as living, breathing symbols of peace, love and freedom – and you certainly shouldn't let me stop you doing so – but the truth is, sadly, rather more prosaic. There were isolated records of the bird from the mid-nineteenth century onwards, presumably escapees that had originally been brought back from the far reaches of the Empire, but there were no records of breeding until the late 1960s or early 1970s, and even then it was another twenty years before the population really started to expand. Over the same period, parakeets started to appear around other European cities as well, suggesting that the real reason for their presence was the carelessness of certain cage-bird owners, or perhaps even deliberate releases. There seem to have been further points of genesis for the UK population, too: parakeets that have slowly established themselves in cities such as Birmingham and Manchester are likely to have nothing at all to do with the London-based birds.

Coming up with a population figure is hard – some estimates are as low as eight thousand pairs, while others range upwards of fifty thousand birds. Given the size of some of the London roosts, it's probably nearer the latter. Esher Rugby Club, for example, has long been known as *the* place to go to see these raucous, roistering creatures bickering and bantering as they settle down for the night, with over six thousand birds at a time using it as their base for commuting throughout the metropolis; while my friend David Lindo, the Urban Birder of TV fame, talks of roosts of two thousand or so at his home patch of Wormwood Scrubs. That, in its way, is even more extraordinary, given that on a clear evening the shining towers and shards of central London look close enough to touch from the Scrubs' central high ground; to see a mass of parakeets flashing across the London Eye, or the Post Office Tower, is to experience a sudden dizzying cognitive dissonance, as though two widely separated points on the planet had suddenly become coexistent.

But it's Sunday lunchtime and I've done all the dizzying I want to do this side of an Australian Shiraz. I watch our little flock of bright-green fly high, wide and handsome, not to mention fast, before descending again towards distant gardens. These, and the British public's willingness to feed garden birds, have been a major cause of their success; and there's heated debate as to whether the parakeets are having an impact on native species, particularly fellow hole-dwellers such as woodpeckers. The jury's still out, and I can't help hoping that they manage to avoid the fate of another escapee and colonist, the ruddy duck, which is all but gone from the UK after a controversial cull designed to protect the white-headed ducks of Spain. The fact that there was little evidence that British ducks were going over there and hybridising, and that, if they did, it would have been easier to cull them in Spain, didn't deter Defra, the Department for the Environment, Food and Rural Affairs.

Were the parakeets to be culled, we'd lose a lot more than just their bright colours and their hugely evocative calls (they're another favourite of TV and film producers). We'd be doing a disservice, I think, to some of nature's great survivors, and losing sight of the fact that practically no species in the modern world lives in isolation from mankind and the good and ill we bring with us. Why does the fact that the parakeets and mandarins were brought here make them any less 'natural' than the waxwings with their reliance on our supermarkets and car parks, or even emblematic British species such as the skylark or blackbird, beneficiaries of our clearance of forests and creation of cultivated areas? Isn't it better to accept that, sometimes, we're also responsible for happy accidents? No one wants an unrestrained traffic of alien species into sensitive habitats, but we play God at our peril, and we'd do well to remember that no one can foresee all the consequences of any given action.

14  Silver Linings

In the half-light of dawn the only birds to be seen are half-a-dozen oystercatchers, hunched here and there on the far bank of the gravel pit. The black and white plumage that gave them their folk-name of 'sea-pie' makes them stand out in virtually any context, and just for good measure each of them has a bill that resembles nothing so much as the carrot used for a snowman's nose.

Snowmen. There'll be a few of them before the day is through, inland at least, because the wind has turned round and is blowing straight out of the north. With nothing to get in its way between the Arctic and the north Norfolk coast, it goes to work, defining the phrase 'chilled to the bone'. Back along the sea wall, and among the caravans and chalets back towards the main road, nothing's moving. Anyone with a choice in the matter will be staying in bed a couple of hours longer.

I'm grateful for the cover and the little bit of warmth that the hide provides, and I start scanning through the birds closest to hand, a mixture of ducks such as mallards, goldeneye and the odd pintail, and waders such as dunlin and redshank on the bank just below me. I am, I admit, slightly baffled as to where the hundreds of waders I'd watched skimming low over the sea wall and into the pits not fifteen minutes ago have gone, but I assume they're in the next pit.

I've been here fully five minutes before I raise the binoculars to take a close look at that far bank, and as I do one of the oystercatchers starts to move down towards the water. Then the whole bank seems to move, with the small, uniformly grey boulders that are part of it separating to let the bird pass. And then I realise – and only the combination of the cold and the early start is any excuse for my foolishness – that every one of those boulders is a bird.

A knot to be exact. With each of them standing stock still in the same position, head tucked away and little but a grey expanse of wing and back showing, they were creatures of stone, but the bigger, black-and-white bird's intrusion into their silent vigil softens them again suddenly into a single seething mass of avian life.

I try counting them, but I give up long before they start to pose any threat to my state of wakefulness. They stay obligingly still but there are so many. Given the numbers I can count, packed into an area roughly ten feet by ten feet, I estimate I'm looking at seven or eight thousand, on this pit alone. Seven or eight thousand tiny Cnuts – one theory is that their name derives from that of the eleventh-century monarch who told the sea to turn back – just biding their time before they can return to the nearby mudflats and order the tide to retreat.

In fact, there are other waders amongst them too – dunlin and redshanks again – but for the most part each species sticks to its own little area. If you were so minded, you could teach yourself a decent amount about the finer points of winter wader ID, but that would be to lose sight of a wider picture that's unique in Britain – unique pretty much anywhere. Snettisham RSPB reserve has made its name and become a magnet for wildlife photographers, partly by design and partly by accident, and its greatest glories depend on the rare conjunction of a number of factors. When they fall into alignment there's little to match it.

So much of the landscape of Britain has been shaped and tamed by man that we tend to forget the strange and wonderful shapes it must once have taken. The Wash, that great bite out of England's east coast, is our biggest river delta, for all that it now looks nothing like our stereotypical image of that word.

If you visit the Wash expecting sparkling channels of water threading through stands of reeds and rushes, the air thick with the shapes and calls of egrets, storks and flamingos, then forget it. Well, except the egrets maybe. No, this area is a delta shaped and tamed by man. Rivers run down dead-straight miles, through sluice and lock, to emerge onto wide mudflats. Between them, huge fields of black soil are punctuated by dykes and bunds, the occasional hedge, and little farms huddled behind flimsy spinneys, the only cover against a wind that can arrive straight from the Urals.

For many centuries this delta formed a key access point for migrants and invaders set on making Britain their home. Archaeological discoveries at Snettisham have uncovered early Anglo-Saxon villages, and common sense dictates that settlers arriving from northern Germany and Denmark would have headed straight for sites such as this, almost adjacent to the open sea to make retreat possible, yet close enough to a host of major rivers to make penetration into the heart of the island a possibility. From the Wash, the Ouse, the Nene and the Welland are highways to the English Midlands, the 'champaine ground' as one medieval chronicler was to call it, that would eventually be a major foundation of the country's wealth.

And while some passed on into the interior of England, others remained, settled down and lived in this landscape, which must have felt reassuringly home-like for those who had arrived from Jutland and the like. As they converted to Christianity, another enduring feature of the Fens emerged, the great cathedrals and abbeys of Ely, Ramsey, Thorney, Crowland and Peterborough, like great grey ships breasting seas of green.

Later, Viking armies intent on harvesting the riches of those great churches sailed their dragon-prowed ships into the same muddy estuaries, only to be gradually absorbed into the country in the same way. But the landscape remained the same. When Hereward the Wake led resistance to William the Conqueror from the Isle of Ely in 1070, Ely really was an island, a small, raised area amidst a trackless wilderness of rivers, channels, marshes and pools, and the rebel had high hopes that his insurrection would be supported by the ships and men of the Danish king Sweyn, who could sail right up to the city if need be. He was to be disappointed, but even in the centuries following the Conquest little changed, with the fen-dwellers developing their own distinctive way of life that made good use of the natural riches – both piscine and avian – available to them.

It wasn't a healthy place to live, admittedly. The ague, as malaria and similar feverish diseases were then known, was a constant threat, and it's a mark of how difficult travel across the boggy, treacherous country was that King John lost some or all of the crown jewels in the whirlpools and quicksands of the estuaries in 1216. No one knows exactly where, but legend has it that there's a fortune out there waiting to be found.

Eventually someone did make a fortune out of this distinctly unpromising countryside. A Dutchman by the name of Cornelius Vermuyden. In the seventeenth century, a growing population and the burgeoning economic and political power of the gentry meant that there was ever-increasing pressure to bring more land into cultivation, or under enclosure for sheep and other livestock. Marginal upland pastures were walled and fenced. Others disappeared beneath the plough. By far the greatest untapped riches, though, in terms of land, were the wide acres of the Fens, stretching from up near Skegness in the north down to near Cambridge in the south, and from King's Lynn in the east to Peterborough in the west.

Vermuyden, with other engineers from the Low Countries, applied centuries of accumulated expertise to drain the mires and swamps, although their efforts met with any number of setbacks and even active opposition, and the process wasn't completed until well into the eighteenth century. Since then the drainage has been refined and perfected, until the whole area is probably the richest and most productive agricultural land in the UK. As with other places where intensification of farming has taken place, this hasn't always been good for birds, although a winter afternoon on the Fens can produce a surprising wealth of avian life.

This includes not only the flocks of lapwings, golden plovers, gulls and corvids, or the barn owls hunting wide field verges and making use of the many abandoned outbuildings (the bleakness of the landscape, perhaps, has reined in the renovations and conversions that are so prevalent elsewhere). There are corn buntings, for example: chunky, seed-eating passerines once widespread across arable land but now struggling badly in most other parts of the country. There are marsh harriers, only thirty years ago a major rarity, yet now revived to the extent that seeing one from my office window at the edge of Peterborough isn't a huge surprise. There are even cranes, long-necked, plumed and exotic, and finally making a strong comeback in a country whose place names tell the story of their abundance as both breeders and passage migrants in centuries past. These range from Cranborne ('cranes' stream') in Dorset, to Carnforth ('cranes' ford') in Lancashire.

Nonetheless, birds aren't here in anything like the vast quantities they would be were this still the delta of our imaginations. Only on the far side of the earthen sea walls that line the Wash can you find anything on the scale of the world's great wetlands. The greys and browns of the huge sea of mud might not be of the right hues to inspire painters or poets, but they do harbour an astonishing amount and variety of life, from microscopic organisms to larger crustaceans such as crabs. All of these are food to birds of one sort or another, and so these empty and often bleak surroundings exert an irresistible pull on avian life from as far afield as the Arctic.

As autumn draws on, birds arrive daily. Pink-footed geese from Iceland, perhaps fresh from a stop-off in Scotland. Bar-tailed godwits from the same location, besides other waders such as knot and dunlin from the tundra of Svalbard, Greenland and elsewhere. Short-haul travellers, too, from the uplands of Britain: curlews and golden plovers, determined to take advantage of the daily feast on offer, rather than the slim pickings to be found on their breeding grounds during the winter months. Even some of the waders found around our coasts at all times of the year – oystercatchers, for example – find it hard to resist the magnetic pull of this incredible place.

For day after day it fills with birds, large and small, some easily seen, and others content to live their lives far from man, way out on the mud; but it takes a coming together of two natural phenomena to reveal to even the casual observer the sheer scale of what's out there.

You need to do your research. This is one of those natural spectacles than can genuinely only be seen to its fullest extent on one or two days each year, and so getting your timing even slightly wrong is a recipe for disappointment.

First of all, you need all the requisite birds to be present. That means waiting until late December at least, because some of our winter visitors can take their time to get here, especially in a mild year. On the other hand, by the end of January some of the visitors might be starting to slip away to the north, especially those species that tend to make their return journey in stages. That means you're working with a window of six weeks at most.

Secondly, you need a day on which high tide and dawn pretty much coincide – cross-reference that with your six-week window, and you've generally got a couple of suitable days, usually in early or mid-January.

Finally, as with absolutely any outdoor event that takes place in Britain, from the humblest church fete to the Lord's Test match or Wimbledon, you need the weather. Fog, mist and drizzle all have the potential to obscure the extent of what's happening, but clear days and nights have their own hazards, too. In the end, all you can do is hope, and having made all my calculations that's what I do.

I've risen long before dawn and driven along the coast road from where I'm staying near the RSPB reserve at Titchwell. It's bitterly cold, mainly due to the biting wind, and the skies are largely clear with just some high cloud away to the west. The moon is still riding high, almost three-quarters full and casting a silver sheen across the sage-green fields lining the lane from Snettisham village.

That worries me. Pink-footed geese are a key part of what I'm hoping to see, but they're far from reliable in their movements. In recent decades the numbers wintering in Britain have increased markedly, in part because of their breeding success in Iceland and eastern Greenland, but also because they've found the farmland of Britain more and more welcoming. In some areas, such as north-east Scotland, they'll feed mainly on stubble fields, but in East Anglia, and especially north Norfolk, their expansion since the Second World War was heavily linked to one crop – sugar beet. Once harvested the beet tops were left lying on the fields and the geese were happy to exploit this ample and energy-rich food resource. It helped, too, that the fields of East Anglia tend to be large and wide open, often without hedges, which suits this rather nervous bird perfectly – there's little or no chance of a predator making a close approach unnoticed. Having fed on the fields inland throughout the day, the geese of north Norfolk return to coastal roost sites at night, either at Holkham or on the Wash near Snettisham.

But, and it's a big but, catching them when they return to their roosts is just a best-case scenario for the birdwatcher. Sometimes if the weather's fine and the moon casts enough light the geese will stay on the fields all night, taking advantage of the conditions to feed up while the going's good. This is exactly what I'm afraid of, but there's no way of knowing what will happen until I get down to the sea wall.

In the car park at Snettisham I pull up alongside three others, presumably here for the same reason as me. As I'm taking my scope and binoculars out of the boot, and adding a final extra layer and thick gloves to my winter outfit, a barn owl bobs across the track on its own little tide of silence. So intent is it on the rough grassland separating the parking bays that for a moment I think it's going to fly straight into me, but at around five yards away it lifts it head long enough to detect my presence and veers left, at the same time lifting a yard higher into the air, as if on invisible strings. It disappears into the darkness, and as I follow its path I can see it's not the only bird out and about in the pre-dawn hour. On the grassy fields curlews are probing for worms with their extraordinarily long, curved bills, paying similarly little heed to this lone birdwatcher trudging past.

I walk down a gravel path between holiday chalets as the first slivers of dawn start to streak the eastern horizon. Somewhere in the distance I can hear a faint but growing clamour of many birds, and I start to hurry on, worried that I've got my timings wrong and will miss the show. And yet, while the sound gets louder as I get closer to the sea wall, it never quite builds to a crescendo. There's always the sense there's yet more to come, and I comfort myself that the loudest voices – redshank and black-headed gull – are not the ones I'm really here for.

By the time I'm clambering up onto the wall itself, there's enough light to see for maybe a mile in every direction – mist and fog are mercifully absent – and within five minutes that range has extended to the very far edge of the Wash. From where I am, on its eastern shore, my binoculars can pick out landmarks over on the Lincolnshire coast, such as Boston Stump, another of those great fenland churches that have been actual and spiritual beacons for hundreds of years. Rather more prosaically the great bulk of Sutton Bridge Power Station. And all along the shore as it sweeps right round towards me, the lights marking each of the main channels, where the rainwater of a third of England pours itself into the ocean.

On the mud itself ... nothing. Not with the first scan, or the second; or at least, nothing more than a mottling of the browns and greys with darker or lighter browns and greys. They could be birds, but they could be different-coloured mud, or creeks, or cloud shadow. I start to feel that strange, subdued panic that afflicts every birdwatcher (or maybe it's just me) when they've gone looking for something in particular – the feeling that it's simply too much to ask that your presence and the presence of the bird or birds should coincide out there in all that space.

And then, beyond doubt, something is moving. Small, dark, wispy clouds start to rise from the water's edge, like djinn from desert sands, and beyond them larger shapes, too. Everything, it seems, is happening at once.

In fact, dawn has the edge on this occasion. The larger shapes are the pink-footed geese, and the increasing light sends small groups of them spiralling into the sky, from where they strike out directly towards me in wide V-formations. I'm still worried that some may have spent the night inland, and that the scale of the spectacle will be massively diluted, but I start to follow the leading skeins with my binoculars anyway.

As they get closer I can see the small, dark, rounded heads, the shortish necks and compact overall shape, the dark underwings and the white edge to the tail, and as they get closer still their voices join the general clamour. In flight they keep up a constant chorus of urgent, high-pitched disyllabic calls – ang-ank, ang-ank, ang-ank – to each other.

It's dangerous to assume we can ever know exactly what bird calls mean, but with all geese in flight I am given the impression that this is the sound of reassurance and encouragement, a sort of 'all for one and one for all' proclamation to the rest of the flock to reinforce bonds of mutual dependence.

And there's scientific backing for ideas along these lines: certainly geese adopt those V-formations precisely because the trailing birds receive an aerodynamic boost from the updraughts of the wings of those in front of them, with more experienced birds leading the way to ensure the flock has the best possible chance of reaching its destination safely and quickly. Even the lead geese are rotated on a regular basis, ensuring that every bird benefits from being part of the group.

So engrossed have I become in watching one particular group of pathfinders that, when I lower my binoculars to give my arms a rest, I'm staggered. Beyond them hundreds and thousands more geese have risen from the floor of the great bay and are forming up to head east.

For the next fifteen minutes I stand with my head craned skywards as skein after skein passes over to the accompaniment of its own strangely invigorating music (geese will never win prizes for tunefulness, but after a while it's hard not to get caught up in their enthusiasm and sheer joie de vivre). And I count. It's too cold to make notes on my phone, and even gripping a pencil might be a stretch – certainly here bare hands are a hugely unappealing prospect. So I keep the tally in my head, as best as I can, first adding in groups of ten and then, as the birds come thicker and faster, in fifties and even hundreds. And, if the final result does depend heavily on the ability to estimate numbers across a 180-degree arc of sky simultaneously, I'm quietly confident that my final total of fourteen thousand is no more than a few hundred out.

Think of that. Fourteen thousand birds, each of them only a little smaller than the typical farmyard goose, passing two to three hundred feet overhead in the space of fifteen minutes, all of them noisily eager to be about the short day's business of foraging across the flint-spackled fields of Norfolk.

What feels extraordinary is that such huge numbers of this relatively large bird can spend up to six months of the year in a small corner of Britain without, apparently, attracting a great deal of attention, except from incomers like myself. Of course, the locals must inevitably get used to their presence, in much the same way that someone living next to an airport soon ceases to look up at the sound of every aircraft; but nevertheless you do find yourself wondering why there aren't cars pulled over along every main road, with the drivers staring open-mouthed at a truly staggering wildlife movement.

I watch until the last birds have become tiny specks in the eastern sky, then vanish below the horizon, their clangour faded to a faint rumour above the calls of waders and the growing tinnitus of the awakening world. They'll probably be back tonight, of course, but they won't necessarily return in one large movement. The early bird really is the one who gets the early bird.

If geese were all Snettisham had to offer, it would still be utterly worth rising at an unearthly hour and risking hypothermia. But they're not, and what follows can, depending on your view of gangly, gawky shorebirds, make the pink-feet seem like little more than the competent but essentially commonplace opening act of the greatest show you ever saw.

There's a little gaggle of birdwatchers around me now. We were all present to see the geese, but strung out along the sea wall at intervals of around thirty yards or so. Being British our natural reserve demands that we gravitate towards each other only very slowly, and seemingly reluctantly, but the extreme cold probably helps encourage our coming together, seeing as how we're all looking for the slightest excuse to move around and keep warm. Once we do, we start to discuss excitedly what we've just seen, like the audience at a West End musical pouring out into the bar at the interval, talking about highlights from the first half and wondering how on earth the cast are going to top that in the second half.

But top it they do. Where they differ from the stars of the stage is that, taken individually, none of these birds is necessarily stellar. It's just that brought together for the greatest crowd scene of the British birdwatching year, every one of them is unforgettable.

It starts with redshanks. They're familiar enough to birdwatchers of most types and abilities, their extreme sensitivity to danger (especially in the form of man) having long ago earned them the nickname of 'warden of the marshes'. Generally solitary, they start to arrow a few feet over the sea wall, flying straight down the slipstream of their mournful, liquid, three-note whistles – by the time you hear it they're past you.

Golden plovers, too, are birds that still breed in Britain in reasonable numbers, and at least some of those that we see spangling high above the water in the first rays of the risen sun will have made the relatively short journey from the Pennines, or Scotland. In this light they come closer than most to being heavenly bodies, toggling between tiny, almost invisible white dwarfs as they present us with their pale bellies, then exploding into a hundred supernovas of yellow-gold as the flock turns and their backs and wings catch the sun. There are three such groups, with two occasionally combining and then separating again, and they alternate a seemingly aimless wide circling with fast, purposeful flight in our direction, all the time losing height.

Dunlin and knot, on the other hand, are rather less familiar birds, especially for any birder from a landlocked county, like me. In spring and summer they'd be a completely different story, the former resplendent in black waistcoat and rufous back, and the latter a dazzling terracotta shade that outweighs the rather ungainly impression given by its portly outline, as well as fully justifying the species' American moniker of red knot.

For now, though, both are clouds of dark-grey specks in the distance, like so many midges in summertime. Where the golden plovers are creatures of light, these waders seem to be soaking it up. Their flocks twist and gyre like those fractal screen-saver displays on PCs in the 1990s, threatening to tear apart and disintegrate completely, before suddenly coalescing again and taking on a new form. It's truly hypnotic, and again it's easy not to notice that as we watch, they're getting closer, and lower.

Just as it seems they must run out of mudflat over which to perform their perfectly choreographed moves, there's an interruption in their aerial dervish dance. A large female peregrine appears from behind us, flying into the wind with powerful strokes that clearly show her flexed carpal joints. She soars for a few metres every now and then, presumably eyeing the immense moveable feast below and ahead, and the flocks tighten and tighten until they're solid black. The waders know the deep-chested, muscular shape of the raptor for what it is – sudden and violent death – and react accordingly. This, after all, is what flocks are really all about. On its own, not one of those birds would stand a chance against the falcon and her breakneck fury, but together they're something more intimidating. It takes only a few seconds and then the

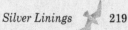

peregrine decides that discretion is the better part of valour, and starts to drift around the shore towards Lincolnshire, perhaps looking to pick off one of the lone curlews that are studding what's left of the mud, or else thinking about heading inland to make a breakfast of woodpigeon.

The peregrine's departure is the signal that the dunlin, golden plovers and especially knots have been waiting for. Birds are unravelled from the larger tangle by invisible forces of kinship, habit and hunger, and are spun out into long thin strands above our heads, before finally snagging on some invisible hook just beyond the gravel pits and falling to earth. But others are emboldened to strike out on their own, perhaps deciding that a faster, more direct approach is needed to secure the best positions at the roost. As we stand birds start to skim lower and lower over our heads, sometimes so close that we feel the draught from their wings as they rush by. Our ears are filled with the strange music – melancholy and yet so urgent that it's life-affirming – of shorebirds calling to each other to remain in contact. Who knows? Calling to the whole world to tell it that they've survived another winter night.

This little squall of birds gathers pace, until you feel as though you could grab a couple simply by raising your outstretched hands above your head. It's a moment to be glad that you made the effort to get up so early and, birds' digestive systems being what they are, relieved that you wore a hat, but most of all it's time to be astonished by the sheer size and scale and the power of crowds.

When, finally, the amount of incoming birds lessens and then stops almost entirely, we make our way to the hide overlooking the nearest gravel pit. After the immense relief at being out of the stinging wind has worn off, and we've begun thinking about using our binoculars again, we're jabbering away once more, so much so that none of us registers exactly what is before us. No one actually says 'where have they all gone to', but we're all thinking it, and it's only when that oystercatcher starts barging his way to the front that we realise we're looking at a landscape made up entirely of birds. While the water's empty enough, pretty well every inch of solid ground in sight is occupied by a wader of one sort or another.

That takes some getting your head around, and again I start marvelling at the fact that this is all happening, not in some distant, remote and picturesque location, but round the back of a humdrum caravan park just a couple of miles from the main roads and filling stations, retail parks and housing estates of the modern world.

Then it strikes me. However deliciously thrilling that juxtaposition is for us – the grandeur of untamed nature next to the gentle, unchanging banality of everyday life – for the birds this is nothing special at all. The waders will have cared nothing for the fact that their own movements were synchronous with those of the geese. The geese likewise. This immense gathering is, to the average knot or dunlin, no more significant than any other. They're used to flying in flocks, feeding in flocks, and breeding in close proximity, and the timing of tides and sunrises are utterly irrelevant. For them the location is neither unspoiled nor man-made, just a huge, muddy fly-through takeaway with adjoining waiting areas to be used for as long as necessary until the next biological imperative wings them halfway across the country, or continent, or world.

And that, perhaps, is the single thing that makes birdwatching so endlessly involving. However much we can predict behaviour based on careful study and past experience, there's no getting away from the fact that every bird is an individual, sentient being with its own motives and particular habits and routines. And while each of them is also affected by mankind's behaviour – above all the destruction of vast swathes of habitat – many are also capable of adapting to new circumstances, or else of arranging their lives so that they intersect with man's only when it's absolutely necessary. The power of flight, of course, gives them more freedom than just about any other creature on the planet and it also invests each encounter with every bird with an aura of good fortune.

Those intersections are what continue to delight me, after getting on for forty years of birding. More than that, they astonish me, in the genuine sense of the word. Even a sighting of a familiar bird – a song thrush riffing from the top of the garden rowan, say – feels like a gift once you take into account that it had so many other places it could be, and so many other things it could be doing. Multiply that feeling and that possibility by tens, and hundreds, and thousands, as so many of the experiences in this book have done, and you can start to feel like the luckiest person on the planet.

Acknowledgements

For help and inspiration, thanks are due to: *Bird Watching* magazine, the RSPB, the Wildfowl & Wetlands Trust, the British Trust for Ornithology, Alison Brackenbury, the Grant Arms in Grantown-on-Spey, Heatherlea Birdwatching Holidays, Knepp Castle Estate, the Wildlife Trusts, Leicestershire and Rutland Ornithological Society, Nine Arches Press, Tim Appleton, Stuart Winter, David Lindo, Rutland Osprey Project, Rick and Elis Simpson, David Morley, John Miles, Mark Cocker, Conor Jameson, Paul Brook, Swarovski Optik, Neil Glenn, Waveney River Centre.

Index

Field Notes From the Edge
Journeys Through Britain's Secret Wilderness

Paul Evans searches out the wildlife and plants that thrive in places such as ridgeways, marshlands, riversides and ditches. Weaving together natural history, art and literature, philosophy and folklore, he explores the secret wilderness that has shaped Britain, revealing a Nature that is inspiring yet intimidating and miraculous yet mundane.

ISBN: 9781846044571
Order direct from www.penguin.co.uk

Also available from Rider

Pathlands
21 Tranquil Walks Among the Villages of Britain

PETER
OWEN JONES

Pathlands

21 TRANQUIL
WALKS
AMONG THE
VILLAGES
OF BRITAIN

Peter Owen Jones explores twenty-one circular walks spanning
the British Isles – from Suffolk to Shropshire, from Cornwall
to Ceredigion. Whether wandering along ancient pilgrim trails,
through leaf-dappled bridleways or converted railway routes,
whether followed with the feet or with heart, the walks in this
book offer space in which to unwind and find calm.

ISBN: 9781846044441
Order direct from www.penguin.co.uk